Altra Veduta dell'avanzo dell'Arco

ROME

A Collection of the Poetry of Place

Edited by
GLYN PURSGLOVE

For Celia & Jess

love

B

ELAND • LONDON

ISBN 978 1 906011 22 2

First published in October 2008 by Eland Publishing Ltd,
61 Exmouth Market, Clerkenwell, London EC1R 4QL

Pages designed and typeset by Antony Gray
Printed and bound in Spain by
GraphyCems, Navarra

CONTENTS

Introduction 9

Arriving in Rome 13

Rome as Seen by the Ancient Romans 25

The Ruins of Rome 43

The Colosseum 63

The Churches of Rome 75

Death, Rome and the English Romantic Poets 91

The Popular Tradition 105

Modern Rome 115

Leaving the City 127

Index of Poem Titles 137

Index of Authors and Translators 139

Acknowledgements 141

INTRODUCTION

Nature is Roman, and mirrored in Rome.
We see its forms of civic grandeur
In transparent air, like a sky-blue circus,
In the forum of fields, in the colonnades of trees.

Nature is Roman, and it seems
Pointless to trouble any gods again:
There are sacrificial entrails to foretell war,
Slaves to keep silence, stones to build!

OSIP MANDELSHTAM (1891–1938),

Translated by James Greene

There seem to be almost as many poems about Rome as there are
about Nature. No city in the world can rival this sheer abundance.
For more than two thousand years poets have been writing
about the city's origins, about the Roman Republic and the
Roman Empire, about the Christian martyrs of Rome, about the
Fall of Rome, about the Pope and the Church – and about much,
much else. Initially the poets wrote in Latin. Later they wrote
about Rome in every European language – and in non-European
languages too.

The resulting body of work is enormous. No collection – even
one much bigger than this – could hope to represent it fairly. In
making the present selection I have largely chosen poems which
relate to particular sites or sights – so that the reader might read
them in location, as it were, actually or in his or her memory and
imagination. This has meant the relative neglect of, for example,

poems which reflect more generally on Rome's politics and history and of narrative poems. Though I have given particular prominence to English-language poets, work in translation is also included. Where no other credit is given, translations are my own.

In the *Paradise Regained* of John Milton (1608–74), Satan presents to Christ a vision of 'an imperial city', tempting Him with the prospects of earthly power:

FROM *Paradise Regained*

John Milton

> With towers and temples proudly elevate
> On seven small hills, with palaces adorned,
> Porches and theatres, baths, aqueducts,
> Statues and trophies, and triumphal arcs,
> Gardens and groves presented to his eyes . . .

Satan explains and identifies the city:

> The city which thou seest no other deem
> Than great and glorious Rome, queen of the earth
> So far renowned, and with the spoils enriched
> Of nations; there the capitol thou seest
> Above the rest lifting his stately head
> On the Tarpeian rock, her citadel
> Impregnable, and there mount Palatine
> The imperial palace, compass huge, and high
> The structure, skill of noblest architects,
> With gilded battlements, conspicuous far,
> Turrets and terraces, and glittering spires.
> Many a fair edifice besides, more like
> Houses of gods (so well I have disposed

My airy microscope) thou mayst behold
Outside and inside both, pillars and roofs
Carved work, the hand of famed artificers
In cedar, marble, ivory or gold.

Milton himself recorded how, in 1638, he spent two months in
Rome, 'viewing the antiquities of that renowned city'. He was
there again at the end of the year and in the early part of 1639
when, he also recorded, 'for about the space of two months I
openly defended the reformed religion in the very metropolis of
popery'. What Milton saw and heard in Rome fascinated and
repelled him (it is no accident that memories of St Peter's seem
to inform his presentation of Pandemonium in Book One of
Paradise Lost) in almost equal measure.

Poetic responses to Rome – like those to Nature, one might
say – are necessarily complex.

ARRIVING IN ROME

'What we had longed so much to see!'

No visitor to Rome can arrive entirely unprepared, entirely without expectations. Medieval pilgrims would have been familiar with the lives of the major Roman saints and with pilgrim guidebooks such as the widely read *Mirabilia Urbis Romae* (*The Wonders of Rome*). The classically educated Grand Tourist of the eighteenth century had read something, at least, of the classical historians and poets. He might also have a book such as *The Voyage of Italy*, a guidebook of 1670, the posthumously published work of Richard Lassels (1603–68), a Catholic priest who often acted as a kind of travelling tutor to those making the 'Grand Tour' (a term which Lassels appears to have coined). The modern visitor comes armed with his choice of guidebook and, no doubt, with images of Rome derived from television and film. The initial arrival involves a measuring of expectations against experience. Many find the reality even more impressive than the mental images with which they came armed. The poet Thomas Gray, arriving in the city (through the Porta del Popolo) in March of 1740, described his arrival in a letter to his mother:

> The first entrance of Rome is prodigiously striking. It is by a noble gate, designed by Michael Angelo, and adorned with statues; this brings you into a large square, in the midst of which is a vast obelisk of granite, and in front you have at one view two churches of a handsome architecture, and so much alike that they are called the twins; with three streets, the middlemost of which is one of the longest in Rome. As high

as my expectation was raised, I confess, the magnificence of this city infinitely surpasses it. You cannot pass along a street but you have views of some palace, or church, or square, or fountain, the most picturesque and noble one can imagine.

Some went so far as to assert that their first encounter with Rome constituted a turning point in their lives. Mary Shelley told one correspondent

> . . . my letter would never end if I were to try to tell a millionth part of the delights of Rome – it has such an effect on me that my past life before I saw it appears a blank and now I begin to live.

A similar image was used by the thirty-seven-year-old Goethe (1749–1832) to describe his own arrival in Rome. Writing on November 1st 1786 he reports excitedly 'at last, I have arrived in the First City of the World!'. A little later, on November 10th, he was describing Rome as a city 'which could never be fully encompassed by the imagination' and was sure that his experience of Rome would leave its mark on all of his future life. His mood was one of rich and varied expectation. He walked from ruin to ruin, gallery to gallery, commented on paintings and sculptures galore. But Rome also stirred in him another kind of expectation, another dimension of the self.

FROM *Roman Elegies*

Goethe

Speak to me, stones, I beg you; you high palaces,
    You streets, utter a word. Genius, do you still sleep?
Life teems within your holy walls, eternal Rome,
    Yet to me alone all stays silent and still. Who first
Will whisper secrets? when first shall I see a fair shape
    At a window, when first burn with quickening love?
Familiar paths will lead me to her and from her,
    Expending hour on hour – but they're unknown as yet.
Still I gaze at church and palace, ruin and column,
    Like any cultured traveller seeing the sights.
Soon this will end, and there'll be a single temple –
    The temple of love, and I a worshipper there.
Rome, you are indeed a world entire – but without
    Love, a world's no world; sans love, Rome would
                    not be Rome.

Goethe's time in Rome was not only a time of cultural and intellectual rebirth; it was also, in all probability, the time of his first successful sexual experiences. In his series of poems known as the *Roman Elegies* he celebrates (though the poems should certainly not be read as direct autobiography) this new sexual awakening, in texts which wonderfully re-vivify the language of such Roman love-elegists as Catullus, Tibullus and Propertius.

Other authors were inspired, by their visits to Rome, to the creation of rather different kinds of texts. A notable example is provided by Edward Gibbon. In his *Memoirs* he records his first arrival in Rome, in 1764:

My temper is not very susceptible of enthusiasm, and the enthusiasm which I do not feel I have ever scorned to affect. But at the distance of twenty-five years, I can neither forget nor express the strong emotions which agitated my mind as I first approached and entered the *eternal City*. After a sleepless night I trod with a lofty step the ruins of the forum; each memorable spot where Romulus *stood*, or Tully spoke, or Caesar fell was at once present to my eye; and several days of intoxication were lost or enjoyed before I could descend to a cool and minute investigation. My guide was Mr. Byers, a Scotch antiquary of experience and taste; but in the daily labour of eighteen weeks the powers of attention were sometimes fatigued, till I was myself qualified in a last review to select and study the capital works of ancient and modern art.

He tells us that

It was at Rome, on the 15th of October 1764, as I sat musing amid the ruins of the Capitol, while the barefooted friars were singing vespers in the temple of Jupiter, that the idea of writing the decline and fall of the city first started to my mind. But my original plan was circumscribed to the decay of the city rather than the empire, and though my reading and reflections began to point toward that object, some years elapsed, and several avocations intervened, before I was seriously engaged in the execution of that laborious work.

Thus was conceived one of the great works of history and one of the masterpieces of English prose: Gibbon's *The Decline and Fall of the Roman Empire* was eventually published in 1788.

An author of more modest achievements, Samuel Rogers (1763–1855) paid his first visit to Rome in November 1814.

Banker, poet and art collector, Rogers was the friend of many more famous poets and writers – from Wordsworth to Dickens. Rogers's diary records his approach to the city, travelling from Florence:

> Went up a hill & were told between the 15th & 16th milestone to prepare for a sight of Rome. Left the Carriage, & ascending, in less than a hundred yards, thro' the haze of the morning & across a dreary and uncultivated plain saw in the horizon what we had longed so much to see! The dome of St Peters, the castle of St Angelo, the *thousand* churches, & the smoke like a light over the rest of the line, tho' the houses were undistinguishable. Rome herself lay before us with all her nameless associations.

In his poem *Italy*, first published anonymously in 1822, Rogers charmingly communicates his excitement at his first experience of the city:

FROM *Italy*

Samuel Rogers

I am in Rome! Oft as the morning-ray
Visits these eyes, waking at once I cry,
Whence this excess of joy? What has befallen me?
And from within a thrilling voice replies,
Thou art in Rome! A thousand busy thoughts
Rush on my mind, a thousand images;
And I spring up as girt to run a race!
    Thou art in Rome! the City that so long
Reigned absolute, the mistress of the world;
The mighty vision that the prophets saw,
And trembled; that from nothing, from the least,

The lowliest village (What but here and there
A reed-roofed cabin by the river side?)
Grew into every thing; and, year by year,
Patiently, fearlessly, working her way
O'er brook and field, o'er continent and sea,
Not like the merchant with his merchandize,
Or traveller with staff and scrip exploring,
But ever hand to hand and foot to foot,
Through nations numberless in battle-array,
Each behind each, each, when the other fell,
Up and in arms, at length subdued them All.

    Thou art in Rome! the City, where the Gauls,
Entering at sun-rise through her open gates,
And, through her streets silent and desolate,
Marching to slay, thought they saw Gods, not men;
The City, that, by temperance, fortitude,
And love of glory, towered above the clouds,
Then fell – but, falling, kept the highest seat,
And in her loneliness, her pomp of woe,
Where now she dwells, withdrawn into the wild,
Still o'er the mind maintains, from age to age,
Her empire undiminished. – There, as though
Grandeur attracted Grandeur, are beheld
All things that strike, ennoble – from the depths
Of Egypt, from the classic fields of Greece,
Her groves, her temples – all things that inspire
Wonder, delight! Who would not say the Forms
Most perfect, most divine, had by consent
Flocked thither to abide eternally,
Within those silent chambers where they dwell,
In happy intercourse? – And I am there!
Ah, little thought I, when in school I sate,

A school-boy on his bench, at early dawn
Glowing with Roman story, I should live
To tread the Appian, once an avenue
Of monuments most glorious, palaces,
Their doors sealed up and silent as the night,
The dwellings of the illustrious dead – to turn
Toward Tibur, and, beyond the City-gate,
Pour out my unpremeditated verse
Where on his mule I might have met so oft
Horace himself – or climb the Palatine,
Dreaming of old Evander and his guest,
Dreaming and lost on that proud eminence,
Long while the seat of Rome, hereafter found
Less than enough (so monstrous was the brood
Engendered there, so Titan-like) to lodge
One in his madness; and inscribe my name,
My name and date, on some broad aloe-leaf,
That shoots and spreads within those very walls
Where Virgil read aloud his tale divine,
Where his voice faltered and a mother wept
Tears of delight!

One of the most interesting of minor Victorian poets, Arthur Hugh Clough (1819–61), finally visited Rome in April 1849. In *Amours de Voyage*, a kind of novel in verse, first published in 1858, Clough's hero, the somewhat immature Oxford don Claude, expresses Clough's impressions of the city.

from *Amours de Voyage*

Arthur Hugh Clough

Dear Eustatio, I write that you may write me an answer,
Or at the least to put us again *en rapport* with each other.
Rome disappoints me much,– St Peter's, perhaps, in especial;
Only the Arch of Titus and view from the Lateran please me:
This, however, perhaps, is the weather, which truly is horrid.
Greece must be better, surely; and yet I am feeling so spiteful,
That I could travel to Athens, to Delphi, and Troy, and
         Mount Sinai,
Though but to see with my eyes that these are vanity also.
 Rome disappoints me much; I hardly as yet
         understand, but
Rubbishy seems the word that most exactly would suit it.
All the foolish destructions, and all the sillier savings,
All the incongruous things of past incompatible ages,
Seem to be treasured up here to make fools of present
         and future.
Would to Heaven the old Goths had made a cleaner
         sweep of it!
Would to Heaven some new ones would come and
         destroy these Churches!
However, one can live in Rome as also in London.
Rome is better than London, because it is other than London.

Only gradually does he qualify his disappointment:

Rome disappoints me still; but I shrink and adapt myself to it.
Somehow a tyrannous sense of superincumbent oppression
Still, wherever I go, accompanies ever, and makes me
Feel like a tree (shall I say?) buried under a ruin of brick-work.
Rome, believe me, my friend, is like its own Monte Testaceo,
Merely a marvellous mass of broken and castaway wine-pots.
Ye gods! what do I want with this rubbish of ages departed,
Things that Nature abhors, the experiments that she
                                        has failed in?
What do I find in the Forum? An archway and two or
                                        three pillars.
Well, but St Peter's? Alas, Bernini has filled it with sculpture!
No one can cavil, I grant, at the size of the great Coliseum.
Doubtless the notion of grand and capacious and massive
                                        amusement,
This the old Romans had; but tell me, is this an idea?
Yet of solidity much, but of splendour little is extant:
'Brickwork I found thee, and marble I left thee!' their
                                        Emperor vaunted;
'Marble I thought thee, and brickwork I find thee!' the
                                        Tourist may answer.

21

Clough himself grew into a recognition of the beauty of Rome, though he remained disturbed by the mingled grandeur and squalor of the city:

FROM *At Rome*

Arthur Hugh Clough

O Land of Empire, art and love!
What is it that you show me?
A sky for Gods to tread above,
A soil for pigs below me!
O in all place and shape and kind
Beyond all thought and thinking,
The graceful with the gross combined,
The stately with the stinking!
Whilst words of mighty love to trace,
Which thy great walls I see on,
Thy porch I pace or take my place
Within thee, great Pantheon,
What sights untold of contrast bold
My ranging eyes must be on!
What though uprolled by young and old
In slumberous convolution
Neath pillared shade must lie displayed
Bare limbs that scorn ablution,
Should husks that swine would never pick
Bestrew that patterned paving,
And sores to make a surgeon sick
For charity come craving?
Though oft the meditative cur
Account it small intrusion
Through that great gate to quit the stir

Of market-place confusion,
True brother of the bipeds there,
If Nature's need requireth,
Lifts up his leg with tranquil air
And tranquilly retireth:
Though priest think fit to stop and spit
Beside the altar solemn,
Yet, boy, that nuisance why commit
On this Corinthian column?

Cees Nooteboom opens *Roads to Santiago*, his superb book on Spain, with an observation on arrivals and departures: 'It is impossible to prove and yet I believe it: there are some places in the world where one is mysteriously magnified on arrival or departure by the emotions of all those who have arrived and departed before.' Rome, inescapably, is one such place, its own history and the history of its visitors so richly multi-layered.

For Lotte Kramer, for example, a child refugee from Hitler's Germany, resident in England since 1939, visiting Rome is inevitably understood by reference to Goethe's time in the city:

On Leaving for Rome with Thoughts about Goethe

Lotte Kramer

Almost in innocence,
So it seems to us now,
Goethe called Rome
The world's capital.

We fly there between
One week and the next,

An event that could change us
Or touch islands.

He worked there at newness
Of seeing, his hunger
Collecting the whole city
With prepared hands.

A summer night, he describes,
With the moon labouring
Through warm yellow mist
'Like an English sun.'

We come from that province
And envy the leisure
He used like love
Assembling passion.

ROME AS SEEN BY THE ANCIENT ROMANS

Asking the price of bread

In the *Aeneid*, his great epic of the origins and destiny of Rome, Virgil (70–19BC) defines what one might think of as the 'official' vision of Roman identity. Its hero Aeneas subordinates (though not without difficulty) his personal desires to the needs and wishes of his people. In a number of 'flash-forwards', Virgil offers quasi-prophetic accounts of Rome's future greatness, of its destined role as an imperial power which would control and civilise other of the earth's peoples. In Book VI of the poem, as Aeneas traverses the underworld, the spirit of Anchises points out Romulus to him, and defines Rome's particular historical destiny:

FROM *The Aeneid*

Virgil

See Romulus the great, born to restore
The crown that once his injured grandsire wore.
This prince, a priestess of your blood shall bear;
And like his sire in arms he shall appear.
Two rising crests his royal head adorn;
Born from a god, himself to godhead born.
His sire already signs him for the skies,
And marks his seat amidst the deities.
Auspicious chief! Thy race in times to come
Shall spread the conquests of Imperial Rome:
Rome whose ascending tow'rs shall heaven invade;
Involving earth and ocean in her shade:

High as the mother of the gods in place;
And proud, like her, of an immortal race…
Let others better mould the running mass
Of metals, and inform the breathing brass;
And soften into flesh a marble face:
Plead better at the bar; describe the skies,
And when the stars descend, and when they rise.
But, Rome, 'tis thine alone, with awful sway,
To rule mankind; and make the world obey;
Disposing peace, and war, thy own majestic way.
To tame the proud, the fetter'd slave to free;
These are imperial arts, and worthy thee.

Translated by John Dryden

For all the greatness of Virgil's work, it is in the poems of some of the other writers of ancient Rome that we encounter a fuller picture of daily life in Rome. Some of these poets are conscious of the gap between the Roman ideal and the Roman reality; others choose to distance themselves from that ideal. The poets' image of life in the imperial city is sometimes angrily satirical, sometimes comfortably amused, sometimes the expression of their own enjoyment of the pleasures made available by the city's wealth and power.

Virgil's younger contemporary Horace (65–8BC) often writes of public affairs but some of his most enduring poems speak, rather, of social pleasures, such as wine and friendship, and of the comforts of the quiet mind. In the unambitious life Horace finds another kind of Roman 'ideal':

FROM *The Satires*

Horace

Alone I wander, as by fancy led,
I cheapen herbs, or ask the price of bread;
I listen, while diviners tell their tale,
Then homeward hasten to my frugal meal,
Herbs, pulses, and pancakes; each a separate plate;
While three domestics at my supper wait.
A bowl on a white marble table stands,
Two goblets, and an ewer to wash my hands;
A hallowed cup of true Campanian clay
My pure libations to the gods to pay.
I then retire to rest, nor anxious fear
Before dread Marsyas[1] to appear,
Whose very statue swears it cannot brook
The meanness of that slave-born judge's look.
I sleep till ten; then take a walk, or choose
A book perhaps, or trifle with the muse:
For cheerful exercise and manly toil
Anoint my body with the pliant oil,
But not with such as Natta's, when he vamps
His filthy limbs, and robs the public lamps.
   But when the sun pours down his fiercer fire,
And bids me from the toilsome sport retire,
I haste to bathe, then decently regale
My craving stomach with a frugal meal,
Enough to nourish nature for a day,
Then trifle my domestic hours away.

---

1   The satyr Marsyas challenged Apollo to a music contest. He lost, and
    was flayed alive for his hubris. A statue of Marsyas stood in the Forum,
    opposite the rostra where judges gave their decisions.

> Such is the life from bad ambition free;
> Such comfort has the man low-born like me;
> With which I feel myself more truly blessed
> Than if my sires the questor's power possessed.

Translated by Philip Francis

One of the loveliest of Horace's odes celebrates the attractions of a warm winter fire, good wine and 'sweet love' (and a view of the highest of the neighbouring mountains):

FROM *The Odes*

Horace

> One dazzling mass of solid snow
>   Soracte stands; the bent woods fret
>   Beneath their load; and, sharpest-set
> With frost, the streams have ceased to flow.
>
> Pile on great faggots and break up
>   The ice: let influence more benign
>   Enter with four-years-treasured wine,
> Fetched in the ponderous Sabine cup.
>
> Leave to the Gods all else. When they
>   Have once bid rest the winds that war
>   Over the passionate seas, no more
> Gray ash and cypress rock and sway.
>
> Ask not what future suns shall bring:
>   Count to-day gain, whate'er it chance
>   To be: nor, young man, scorn the dance,
> Nor deem sweet Love an idle thing,

Ere Time thy April youth had changed
   To sourness. Park and public walk
   Attract thee now, and whispered talk
At twilight meetings pre-arranged;

Hear how the pretty laugh that tells
   In what dim corner lurks thy love;
   And snatch a bracelet or a glove
From wrist or hand that scarce rebels.

Translated by C. S. Calverley

A more aggressively cynical pursuit of 'love' characterises *The Art of Love* by Ovid (43BC–AD17), a sophisticated and witty guide to finding, winning and enjoying a lover. For this young man about town, the monuments and grand entertainments of Rome are chiefly justified by the opportunities they provide. Would-be seducers are advised to pay regular visits to the Circus Maximus, the grandest of Roman venues for chariot racing.

FROM *The Art of Love*

Ovid

The *Capacious Circus*, of a large extent,
Where right-bred horses run, you must frequent;
Point not at all with fingers any way,
Nor with a nod do you your thoughts betray.
Accost your Mistress, whilst by none denied,
And gently join your self unto her side;
If she refuse that you should sit so near,
The custom of the place allows it there;

Here you must ask (for 'tis the readiest way
To gain discourse) things in the present play:
Whose horse is this comes up, and then must you
Whatever she commends, commend it too.
Or when a stately show th' contenders raise,
As you see her, so you must *Venus* praise.
Or if the dust rais'd high fall on her, then
You with your hand must brush it off again.
If none light on her, yet brush off that none,
Action in such a case becometh one.
If her loose mantle fall unto the ground,
To take't up, you must be officious found:
Whilst you stoop low, observe with nimble eye,
If that you can a dainty legge espy.
Take care lest they that sit behind her push,
Or with their knees her tender back should crush.
'Tis profitable slight things please her oft,
As with your hand to make her cushion soft.
Some, fanning cool air, do their Mistress move,
Or with a foot eas'd give a birth to love.
The *Circus* yields such opportunities,
Or th' sand which all about the *Forum* flies.
Oft amorous youths, that on th' *Arena* fought,
Beholding others wounds, worse wounds have caught.

Translated by Francis Wolferston

Elsewhere, Ovid celebrates remembered times of erotic fulfilment:

Ovid

In summer's heat and mid-time of the day,
To rest my limbs upon a bed I lay;
One window shut, the other open stood,
Which gave such light as twinkles in a wood
Like twilight glimpse at setting of the sun,
Or night being past, and yet not day begun.
Such light to shamefast maidens must be shown,
Where they may sport, and seem to be unknown.
Then came Corinna in a long loose gown,
Her white neck hid with tresses hanging down,
Resembling fair Semiramis going to bed,
Or Lais of a thousand wooers sped.
I snatched her gown; being thin, the harm was small,
Yet strived she to be covered therewithal,
And striving thus as one that would be cast,
Betrayed herself, and yielded at the last.
Stark naked as she stood before mine eye,
Not one wen in her body could I spy.
What arms and shoulders did I touch and see,
How apt her breasts were to be pressed by me!
How smooth a belly under her waist saw I,
How large a leg, and what a lusty thigh!
To leave the rest, all liked me passing well;
I clinged her naked body, down she fell.
Judge you the rest: being tired she bade me kiss;
Jove send me more such afternoons as this.

Translated by Christopher Marlowe

In the poems of Catullus (*c*.84–54 BC) and Propertius (*c*.50–*c*.10 BC) love is more often problematic, a source of intense and sometimes troubling feelings and experiences. Propertius, for example, describes a final visit from his beloved Cynthia – a visit paid on the night following her cremation and the interment of her ashes, near Tivoli.

FROM *The Elegies*

Propertius

Ghosts do exist. Death does not finish all.
The colourless shade escapes the burnt-out pyre.
Though lately buried beside the rumbling road,
Yet Cynthia seemed to lean above my bed
When after love's last rites my sleep hung back
And I grieved that my bed was now a chilly realm.
She had the selfsame hair and eyes as on
Her bier, her shroud was burned into her side,
The fire had gnawed at her favourite beryl ring,
And Lethe's water had wasted away her lips.
She breathed out living passion, and spoke,
Yet her brittle hands rattled their thumb-bones.

Forsworn (although no girl should hope for better
From you), can sleep already possess your faculties?
Had waking Suburan[2] secrets, the window-sill worn
By nightly intrigue, already slipped your mind? –

---

2 Subura was a densely populated part of the city, east of the Forum in the low-lying area between the Esquiline and Viminal hills, notoriously noisy and dirty. Tradesmen, craftsmen, prostitutes and pickpockets crowded its narrow streets.

From which for you I've often hung on a rope
And descended hand over hand to your arms!
Often our love was joined in very street,
Heart to heart: our cloaks warmed up the path.
Alas, the secret oaths whose lying words
The South has torn apart and will not heed!

Translated by W. G. Shepherd

The phrase *carpe diem* – 'pluck the day' – was coined by Horace (*Odes*, I. xi) but the same advice, the encouragement (perhaps tactical in the context) to enjoy the available pleasures of the present and not worry overmuch about the future, is memorably expressed in one of Catullus's finest lyrics:

FROM *Carmina*

Catullus

Lesbia[3], live to love and pleasure,
    Careless what the grave may say:
When each moment is a treasure,
    Why should lovers lose a day?

Setting suns shall rise in glory,
    But when little life is o'er,
There's an end of all the story:
    We shall sleep; and wake no more.

3   The Lesbia of Catullus's poems may well have been Clodia, infamously
    promiscuous wife of the aristocrat Q. Caecilius Metellus Celer.

Give me, then, a thousand kisses,
  Twice ten thousand more bestow,
Till the sum of boundless blisses
  Neither we, nor envy know.

Translated by John Longhorne

In a later poem, Catullus displays a rather different attitude in his presentation of Lesbia, addressing his remarks to a friend:

FROM *Carmina*

Catullus

My Lesbia, Caelius, that same Lesbia
Whom once Catullus loved more than himself
And all his own, now in the alleyways
And at street corners milks with a practised hand
The upright members of magnanimous Rome.

Translated by Humphrey Clucas

In the epigrams of Martial (*c.*AD 40–104) we have a wonderfully vivid depiction of many aspects of Roman life in the first century. Martial is capable of the most moving tenderness, as in this elegy for a six-year-old girl:

FROM *The Epigrams*

Martial

> Underneath this greedy stone
> Lies little sweet Erotion;
> Whom the Fates, with hearts as cold,
> Nipp'd away at six years old.
> Thou, whoever thou may'st be,
> That hast this small field after me,
> Let the yearly rites be paid
> To her little slender shade;
> So shall no disease or jar
> Hurt thy house, or chill thy Lar;[4]
> But this tomb here be alone,
> The only melancholy stone.

Translated by Leigh Hunt

4   A Lar was a guardian spirit of a family or a house.

Martial is also the supreme Roman poet of scabrous wit, in poems such as these:

FROM *The Epigrams*

Martial

Friend Cotilus, why can't you wash in
The hip-bath that your comrades splash in?
Is 't 'cause you'll not your lather mix
With creamy streaks from fetid pricks?
If so, next time you take your tub,
Your lower parts you first must scrub.
To give your face the first ablution
Would taint the water with far worse pollution.

Translated by George Sala

I muse not that your Dog turds oft doth eat,
To a tongue that licks your lips, a turd's sweet meat.

Translated by Francis Davison

When *Galla* for her health goeth to the bath,
She carefully doth hide, as is most meet,
With aprons of fine linen, or a sheet,
Those parts, that modesty concealed hath:
Nor only those, but ev'n the breast and neck,
That might be seen or shown, without all checke.
   But yet one foul and unbeseeming place,
   She leaves uncovered still: What's that? Her face.

Translated by Sir John Harington

I would not have a wench with such a waist
As might be well with a thumb-ring embrac'd;
Whose bony hips, which out on both sides stick,
Might serve for graters, and whose lean knees prick;
One, which a saw does in her back-bone bear,
And in her rump below carries a spear.
Nor would I her yet of bulk so gross
That weigh'd should break the scales at th'market-cross;
A mere unfathom'd lump of grease; no, that
Like they that will; 'tis flesh I love, not fat.

Translated by Sir Edward Sherburne

There are many other sides to Martial, many other images of
Roman life which he offers us. He evokes, for example, a world of
sociability and friendship grounded in the realities of life in the
city, as in the following poem, which provided the groundwork
for Ben Jonson's seventeenth-century poem 'Inviting a Friend to
Supper':

FROM *The Epigrams*

Martial

Trimly to sup, *Julius,* I thee invite:
If better be not offer'd, come tonight.
We'll bathe together, at six a clock be here,
Nero's Baths, to my house, you know, are near.
Melons and figs, for ante-past, I'll serve,
Other regalios, which are deemed to have
The grateful properties health to preserve,
And quicken appetite. If you ask, What more?
I'll lie, to make you come. Oysters, wild boar,

37

Choice fatted fowl ta'en from the coop or pens,
Those nobler yet, that range the woods and fens:
Such as ev'n *Stella* rarely does afford,
Tho' altogether princely is his board.
I'll promise more, no verses I'll recite,
To hear yours read, I'll dedicate the night,
Your *Giants War,* your *Art of Tilling Fields,*
Which not in Worth t' immortal *Virgil*'s yields.

Anonymous translation

The Baths of Nero occupied a rectangular area between the Pantheon and the modern-day Piazza Navona (formerly the stadium of Domitian). From a house near there Martial might, like the modern visitor, have made his way across the Tiber, through the lively district of Trastevere and up the Janiculum Hill. For Martial, one reason for making such a journey would have been to visit his friend (and near namesake) Julius Martial:

FROM *The Epigrams*

Martial

My Martial owns a garden, famed to please,
Beyond the glades of the Hesperides;
Along Janiculum lies the chosen block
Where the cool grottos trench the hanging rock.
The moderate summit, something plain and bare,
Tastes overhead of a serener air;
And while the clouds besiege the vales below,
Keeps the clear heaven and doth with sunshine glow.
To the June stars that circle in the skies

The dainty roofs of that tall villa rise.
Hence do the seven imperial hills appear;
And you may view the whole of Rome from here:
Beyond, the Alban and the Tuscan hills;
And the cool groves and the cool falling rills.
Rubre Fidenæ, and with virgin blood
Anointed once Perenna's orchard wood.
Thence the Flaminian, the Salarian way,
Stretch far abroad below the dome of the day;
And lo! the traveller toiling toward his home;
And all unheard, the chariot speeds to Rome!
For here no whisper of the wheels; and tho'
The Mulvian Bridge, above the Tiber's flow,
Hangs all in sight, and down the sacred stream
The sliding barges vanish like a dream,
The seaman's shrilling pipe not enters here,
Nor the rude cries of porters on the pier.
And if so rare the house, how rarer far
The welcome and the weal that therein are!
So free the access, the doors so widely thrown
You half imagine all to be your own.

Translated by Robert Louis Stevenson

The Janiculum remains a place from which some of the very best views of Rome can be enjoyed, and offers rest and (relative) quiet after the noise of the city centre. But it hasn't always been a place of peace – it was here in April 1849 that Garibaldi and his small troop of volunteers held out for two months, in defence of the short-lived Roman Republic, against hugely superior numbers of French troops. A large monument to Garibaldi occupies a prominent place on the hill.

The kind of satisfaction which Martial expresses in these last two poems seems to have eluded the satirist Juvenal (*c*.AD 50–*c*.127) or, at any rate, not to have been part of the persona adopted in his sixteen satires. In the sixth satire he savagely attacks the women of contemporary Rome; as is often the way of the satirist, he contrasts the present state of affairs with a supposedly superior past:

FROM *The Satires*

Juvenal

Once poor, and therefore chaste in former times,
Our matrons were: no luxury found room
In low-roofed houses, and bare walls of loam;
Their hands with labour hard'ned while 'twas light,
And frugal sleep supplied the quiet night.
While pinched with want, their hunger held 'em straight:
When *Hannibal* was hov'ring at the gate:
But wanton now, and lolling at our ease,
We suffer all th' invet'rate ills of peace;
And wasteful riot, whose destructive charms
Revenge the vanquished world, of our victorious arms.
No crime, no lustful postures are unknown;
Since poverty, our guardian-god, is gone:
Pride, laziness, and all luxurious arts,
Pour like a deluge in, from foreign parts:
Since gold obscene, and silver found the way,
Strange fashions with strange bullion to convey,
And our plain simple manners to betray.
What care our drunken dames to whom they spread?
Wine, no distinction makes of tail or head.
Who lewdly dancing at a midnight-ball,

For hot eringoes[5], and fat oysters call:
Full brimmers[6] to their fuddled noses thrust;
Brimmers the last provocatives of lust.
When vapours to their swimming brains advance,
And double tapers on the tables dance.
Now think what bawdy dialogues they have,
What *Tullia* talks to her confiding slave;
At modesty's old statue: when by night,
They make a stand, and from their litters light;
The Good Man early to the levee goes,
And treads the nasty puddle of his spouse.
The secrets of the Goddess named the Good,
Are even by boys and barbers understood:
Where the rank matrons, dancing to the pipe,
Gig with their bums, and are for action ripe;
With music raised, they spread abroad their hair;
And toss their Heads like an enamoured mare:
Laufella lays her garland by, and proves
The mimic lechery of manly loves.
Ranked with the lady, the cheap sinner lies;
For here not blood, but virtue gives the prize.
Nothing is feigned, in this venereal strife;
'Tis downright lust, and acted to the life.

Translated by John Dryden

---

5   Eringoes were the candied roots of the Sea Holly, eaten as a sweetmeat
    and believed to be an aphrodisiac.
6   A brimming cup or goblet.

THE RUINS OF ROME

'Stones piled upon stones'

After the Fall of Rome in the fifth century, the troubled and complex history of the city meant that most of its ancient buildings – save for some which were adapted to Christian use – fell into serious decay, as the population declined. Some served as quarries; some were occupied by the otherwise homeless. In many cases nature took over. In the sixteenth century, before the efforts of humanist scholars and the urban planning of Pope Sixtus V in the 1580s, much of what had been the grandeur of Rome was now a scene of contemporary squalor.

Following the papal schism, when there were rival popes in Avignon and Rome, Martin V was elected as sole pope in 1417. The Rome in which he now presided was a small city with a population of less than twenty thousand, many living in huts and hovels scattered amongst the ruins of the classical city. A Papal Bull of 1425 gives a vivid picture of the conditions:

> Many citizens and inhabitants of Rome and its territory, such as butchers, fishmongers, cobblers, farmers and other artisans who live in the very heart of the most beautiful places in the city and who follow their trades there, have been scattering and concealing animal entrails, heads and feet, bones, blood and skins, rotting meat and fish, waste and excrement, as well as rotting cadavers, into the streets, lanes and piazzas, and into all public and private places. Furthermore, many citizens and inhabitants have dared, outrageously and sacrilegiously, to take over and turn to their own uses streets, lanes, piazzas and other places both private and public, whether they be ecclesiastical or secular.

In the Middle Ages the Forum had become a stone-scattered wasteland; earthquakes and fires, neglect and barbarians, the depredations of those who robbed the lead and metal clamps from the ancient buildings or burned the marble for lime to make cement – all had deprived the place of shape or meaning. Marble and masonry lay in heaps, vegetation covering and distorting most of it. In the sixteenth century it was known as the Campo Vaccino (the Cow Pasture), used for the keeping – and the buying and selling – of cattle. Elsewhere, the Palatine Hill was effectively beyond the reach of those interested in the city's antiquities, the massive palaces of Augustus, Tiberius and Septimus Severus more or less buried beneath burgeoning vegetation.

From the time of Petrarch's visit to Rome in 1337, scholars and men of letters began to make the effort to understand the ruins. Giovanni Guidiccioni (1480–1541), born in Lucca and learned humanist, occupied a number of significant civil and ecclesiastical positions, serving as Bishop of Fossombrone and Papal Nuncio to Spain. In 1535 he was named Governor of Rome and as this sonnet, one of fourteen on Rome past and present, shows, he was much troubled by the state of the city.

To Rome

Giovanni Guidiccioni

Thou noble nurse of many a warlike chief,
Who in more brilliant times the world subdued;
Of old, the shrines of gods in beauty stood
Within thy walls, where now are shame and grief:
I hear thy broken voice demand relief,
And sadly o'er thy faded fame I brood, –
Thy pomps no more, – thy temples fallen and rude, –
Thine empire shrunk within a petty fief.
Slave as thou art, if such thy majesty
Of bearing seems, thy name so holy now,
That even thy scattered fragments adore, –
How did they feel, who saw thee throned on high
In pristine splendour, while thy glorious brow
The golden diadem of nations bore?

Translated by Henry Wadsworth Longfellow

The French poet Joachim du Bellay (1522–60) spent four years in Rome, between 1553 and 1557, in the service of his uncle, the cardinal Jean du Bellay. His time there inspired two collections of sonnets, *Les Antiquités de Rome* and *Les Regrets*. The thirty-two poems which make up *Les Antiquités* reflect the poet's own melancholy as much as they present an image of the contemporary condition of Rome itself. The English poet Edmund Spenser (1552–99) produced versions of the poems from *Les Antiquités* (du Bellay's own poems drew heavily on work by earlier poets) as *Ruins of Rome: by Bellay*. Inner and outer worlds, of poet's soul and decaying structures, are both vividly evoked in the following two sonnets from du Bellay's sequence, in Spenser's translation:

FROM *The Ruins of Rome*

Joachim du Bellay

Thou stranger, which for *Rome* in *Rome* here seekest,
And nought of *Rome* in *Rome* perceiv'st at all,
These same old walls, old arches, which thou seest,
Old palaces, is that which *Rome* men call.
Behold what wreake, what ruin, and what waste,
And how that she, which with her mighty power
Tamed all the world, hath tamed herself at last,
The prey of time, which all things doth devour.
Rome now of *Rome* is th'only funeral,
And only *Rome* of *Rome* hath victory;
Nor aught save *Tiber* hastening to his fall
Remains of all: O world's inconstancy.
 That which is firm doth flit and fall away,
 And that is flitting, doth abide and stay.

Here, the decline and destruction of Rome teaches a lesson, not just about the 'inconstancy' of the world but also about the destructive nature of civil war. In the second sonnet, it is the enduring power of the writings of ancient Rome which gives life and meaning to the crumbling structures, to the mere 'corpse' of the ancient city:

Who lists to see, what ever nature, art,
And heaven could do, O *Rome*, thee let him see,
In case thy greatness he can guess in heart,
By that which but the picture is of thee.
Rome is no more: but if the shade of *Rome*
May of the body yield a seeming sight,
It's like a corpse drawn forth out of the tomb

By magic skill out of eternal night:
The corpse of *Rome* in ashes is entombed,
And her great spirit rejoined to the spirit
Of this great mass, is in the same enwombed;
But her brave writings, which her famous merit
    In spite of time, out of the dust doth rear,
    Do make her Idol through the world appear.

Even in later centuries, much remained neglected and over grown. A few great structures, however, remained to impress and inspire the visitor. As early as 1596 Sir Thomas Chaloner could observe that 'such a rabble of English now roam in Italy'. But numbers were to increase a good deal later. With the development of the Grand Tour, especially in the eighteenth century, more and more visitors came to Rome; more and more artists and architects came to study buildings ancient and modern, paintings and sculptures.

John Dyer (1699–1757), Carmarthenshire-born poet and minor painter, spent a year in Italy in 1724–5, studying and sketching. He was later (1740) to publish *The Ruins of Rome*, a poem of more than 540 lines, structured around a narrative of his ascent of the Palatine Hill. Dyer is aware both of the sense of enduring majesty and the sense of loss as he surveys the scene before him:

FROM *The Ruins of Rome*

John Dyer

Fall'n, fall'n, a silent heap; her heroes all
Sunk in their urns; behold the Pride of Pomp,
The Throne of Nations fall'n; obscur'd in dust;
Ev'n yet majestical: the solemn scene

Elates the soul, while now the rising sun
Flames on the ruins, in the purer air
Tow'ring aloft, upon the glitt'ring plain,
Like broken rocks, a vast circumference;
Rent palaces, crushed columns, rifted moles,
Fanes rolled on fanes, and tombs on buried tombs.

He is aware, too, of his fellow visitors:

. . . Here advent'rous in the sacred search
Of ancient arts, the delicate of mind,
Curious and modest, from all climes resort.

Amongst the many impressive sights to be seen, Dyer responds
with particular joy and passion to the Pantheon, built in the
second century AD and which, in terms of structure, survives
largely intact as one of the masterpieces of world architecture:

And next regard yon venerable dome,
Which virtuous *Latium*, with erroneous aim,
Rais'd to her various deities, and nam'd
Pantheon; plain and round; of this our world
Majestic emblem; with peculiar grace,
Before it's ample orb, projected stands
The many-pillar'd portal: noblest work
Of human skill: here, curious architect,
If thou assay'st, ambitious, to surpass
Palladius, *Angelus*, or *British Jones*,
On these fair walls extend the certain scale,
And turn th' instructive compass: careful mark
How far, in hidden art, the noble plain
Extends, and where the lovely forms commence
Of flowing sculpture: nor neglect to note
How range the taper columns, and what weight
Their leafy brows sustain.

The ruins of Rome, for Dyer, teach a lesson about the end of Roman rule, brought about by 'ease and soft delights':

> Vain end of human strength, of human skill,
> Conquest and triumph, and domain, and pomp,
> And ease, and luxury! O luxury,
> Bane of elated life, of affluent states,
> What dreary change, what ruin is not thine?
> How doth thy bowl intoxicate the mind!
> To the soft entrance of thy rosy cave
> How dost thou lure the fortunate and great!
> Dreadful attraction! While behind thee gapes
> Th' unfathomable gulf where *Ashur* lies
> O'erwhelmed, forgotten; and high-boasting *Cham*;
> And *Elam*'s haughty pomp; and beauteous *Greece*;
> And the great queen of earth, imperial *Rome*.

After the substantial interruption to travel caused by the wars with Napoleon, many were very eager to listen to Shelley's advice:

> Go thou to Rome, – at once the paradise,
> The grave, the city, and the wilderness.

Amongst English Romantic poets, Byron, Shelley, Coleridge and Wordsworth (and for the last months of his life, Keats) all visited Rome. Shelley was first in Rome late in 1818, for just a few days, returning there in March of the following year for a longer visit. He wrote to Thomas Love Peacock of the haunted emptiness of the city:

> The Forum is a plain in the midst of Rome, a kind of desert full of heaps of stones and pits, and though so near the habitations of men, is the most desolate place you can conceive. The ruins of temples stand in and around it, shattered columns and ranges of others complete, supporting cornices

of exquisite workmanship, and vast vaults of shattered domes distinct with regular compartments, once filled with sculptures of ivory or brass. The temples of Jupiter, and Concord, and Peace, and the Sun, and the Moon, and Vesta, are all within a short distance of this spot. Behold the wrecks of what a great nation once dedicated to the abstractions of the mind! Rome is a city, as it were, of the dead, or rather of those who cannot die, and who survive the puny generations which inhabit and pass over the spot which they have made sacred to eternity. In Rome, at least in the first enthusiasm of your recognition of ancient time, you see nothing of the Italians. The nature of the city assists the delusion, for its vast and antique walls describe a circumference of sixteen miles, and thus the population is thinly scattered over this space, nearly as great as London. Wide wild fields are enclosed within it, and there are grassy lanes and copses winding among the ruins, and a great green hill, lonely and bare, which overhangs the Tiber.

After the Colosseum, Shelley's greatest love was for the Baths of Caracalla. The modern visitor to the neatly presented – though still profoundly impressive ruins – will struggle to believe that Shelley is writing of the same place:

These consist of six enormous chambers, above 200 feet in height, and each inclosing a vast space like that of a field. There are, in addition, a number of towers and labyrinthine recesses, hidden and woven over by the wild growth of weeds and ivy. Never was any desolation more sublime and lovely. The perpendicular wall of ruin is cloven into steep ravines filled up with flowering shrubs, whose thick twisted roots are knotted in the rifts of the stones. At every step the aerial pinnacles of shattered stone group into new combinations of effect, and tower above the lofty yet level walls, as the distant mountains change their aspect to one travelling rapidly along the plain. The perpendicular walls . . . surround green and level spaces of lawn, on which some elms have grown, and which are interspersed towards their skirts by masses of the fallen ruin, overtwined with the broad leaves of the creeping weeds. The blue sky canopies it, and is as the everlasting roof of these enormous halls.

But the most interesting effect remains. In one of the buttresses, that supports an immense and lofty arch, which 'bridges the very winds of heaven', are the crumbling remains of an antique winding staircase, whose sides are open in many places to the precipice. This you ascend, and arrive on the summit of these piles. There grow on every side thick entangled wildernesses of myrtle, and the myrletus, and bay, and the flowering laurustinus, whose white blossoms are just developed, the wild fig, and a thousand nameless plants sown by the wandering winds. These woods are intersected on every side by paths, like sheep tracks through the copse-wood of steep mountains, which wind to every part of the immense labyrinth. From the midst rise those pinnacles and masses, themselves like mountains, which have been seen from below. In one place you wind along a narrow strip of weed-grown ruin, on one side is the immensity of earth and sky, on the other a narrow chasm, which is bounded by an arch of enormous size, fringed by the many-coloured foliage and blossoms, and supporting a lofty and irregular pyramid, overgrown like itself with the all-prevailing vegetation. Around rise other crags and other peaks, all arrayed, and the deformity of their vast desolation softened down, by the undecaying investiture of nature. Come to Rome. It is a scene by which expression is over-

powered; which words cannot convey. Still further, winding
up one-half of the shattered pyramids, by the path through
the blooming copsewood, you come to a little mossy lawn,
surrounded by the wild shrubs; it is overgrown with
anemones, wall-flowers, and violets, whose stalks pierce the
starry moss, and with radiant blue flowers, whose names I
know not, and which scatter through the air the divinest
odour, which, as you recline under the shade of the ruin,
produces sensations of voluptuous faintness, like the
combinations of sweet music. The paths still wind on,
threading the perplexed windings, other labyrinths, other
lawns, and deep dells of wood, and lofty rocks, and terrific
chasms. When I tell you that these ruins cover several acres,
and that the paths above penetrate at least half their extent,
your imagination will fill up all that I am unable to express
of this astonishing scene.

Shelley adopted the ruins of the Baths as a place to think and
write. In the Preface to *Prometheus Unbound* he notes that 'this
poem was chiefly written upon the mountainous ruins of the
Baths of Caracalla, among the flowery glades, and thickets of
odoriferous blossoming trees, which are extended in ever
winding labyrinths upon its immense platforms and dizzy arches
suspended in the air. The bright blue sky of Rome, and the effect
of the vigorous awakening spring in that divinest climate, and the
new life with which it drenches the spirits even to intoxication,
were the inspiration of this drama.'

Later in the same century Giosuè Carducci (1835–1907) –
the first Italian to win the Nobel Prize for Literature (in 1906) –
included in his *Odi Barbare* (1877) a richly allusive poem on the
Baths. There are echoes of Horace (in the snow-covered Alban
Hills) and references to the altar devoted to Fever that stood on
the Palatine and to the Rome of Romulus and Remus, sometimes

referred to by the Romans as Roma Quadrata. But in the presence of the British tourist and the passing peasant there are contrasting images of 'modern' Rome:

Facing the Baths of Caracalla

Giosuè Carducci

Dull between the Aventine and the Caelian
clouds are running: wind from the evil plain blows
damp: the Alban Hills in the background stand out
white from a snowfall.

With her green veil raised on her ashy tresses
in the book a lady from Britain looks up
what these Roman walls can be named, that challenge
heaven and time, both.

Thick and fast, continuous, black, all croaking,
crows come pouring in like an endless breaker
onto these two walls, of a monstrous height and
threatening higher.

'Ancient giants,' cry the prophetic birds, or
seem to, harshly, 'why are you trying heaven?'
Heavy down the breeze there arrives a sound of
bells from the Lateran.

And a peasant, pulling his cloak tight about him,
passes, whistling deep in his bass's thick beard,
never looking up. I invoke you, Fever,
god always present:

If you ever loved the wide-open weeping
eyes of mothers and their imploring narrow

arms that beg you, goddess, to leave the lolling
heads of their children –

If you once were pleased by your ancient altar
on the Palatine, when the Tiber still licked
at Evander's hill-town and, sailing home at
sunset between those

hills, the Capitol and the Aventine, the early
civis could look up at Quadrata Roma
smiled on by the sun, as he slowly hummed a
song in Saturnians –

Fever, hear my prayers: Dislodge today's men,
and their small possessions, from this whole precinct.
It's religious fear I express: the goddess
Rome is asleep here.

With the noble Palatine for a pillow,
arms wrapped round the Aventine and the Caelian,
through Capena down to the Appian Way she
spreads her strong torso.

Translated by Alistair Elliot

Wordsworth studied Italian – outside the university system –
while an undergraduate in Cambridge, his tutor being Augustine
Isola, a Milanese political refugee. A walking tour, along with his
university friend Robert Jones, took Wordsworth to northern
Italy, notably to Lakes Como and Maggiore, in the summer
vacation of 1790. A few years later he was studying – and
translating – the poetry of Michelangelo. A second visit to Italy
in 1820 was again limited to northern Italy. It was only in 1837
that, travelling with Henry Crabb Robinson, he was finally able

to visit Rome itself. In the poems contained in *Memorials of a Tour in Italy* (1837) he recorded some of his thoughts and impressions. The most substantial of his Roman poems was, however, written before this visit. For many years Wordsworth had been a keen student of Roman history and antiquities; in 1825 he wrote a poetic study of Trajan's Column, one of the great masterpieces of Roman sculpture. It was dedicated by Hadrian to commemorate Trajan's conquest of the Dacians (in modern Romania) and is covered in a spiral frieze some 200 metres long. Wordsworth's poem – based, no doubt, on engraved images of the column and its frieze – was written to demonstrate to his son the possibilities of the subject when it was set for a university poetry prize!

The Pillar of Trajan

William Wordsworth

Where towers are crushed, and unforbidden weeds
O'er mutilated arches shed their seeds;
And temples, doomed to milder change, unfold
A new magnificence that vies with old;
Firm in its pristine majesty hath stood
A votive Column, spared by fire and flood: –
And, though the passions of man's fretful race
Have never ceased to eddy round its base,
Not injured more by touch of meddling hands
Than a lone obelisk, 'mid Nubian sands,
Or aught in Syrian deserts left to save
From death the memory of the good and brave.
Historic figures round the shaft embost
Ascend, with lineaments in air not lost:

Still as he turns, the charmed spectator sees
Group winding after group with dream-like ease;
Triumphs in sunbright gratitude displayed,
Or softly stealing into modest shade.
– So, pleased with purple clusters to entwine
Some lofty elm-tree, mounts the daring vine;
The woodbine so, with spiral grace, and breathes
Wide-spreading odours from her flowery wreaths.

Borne by the Muse from rills in shepherds' ears
Murmuring but one smooth story for all years,
I gladly commune with the mind and heart
Of him who thus survives by classic art,
His actions witness, venerate his mien,
And study Trajan as by Pliny seen;
Behold how fought the Chief whose conquering sword
Stretched far as earth might own a single lord;
In the delight of moral prudence schooled,
How feelingly at home the Sovereign ruled;
Best of the good – in pagan faith allied
To more than Man, by virtue deified.

Memorial Pillar! 'mid the wrecks of Time
Preserve thy charge with confidence sublime –
The exultations, pomps, and cares of Rome,
Whence half the breathing world received its doom;
Things that recoil from language; that, if shown
By apter pencil, from the light had flown.
A Pontiff, Trajan *here* the Gods implores,
There greets an Embassy from Indian shores;
Lo! he harangues his cohorts – *there* the storm
Of battle meets him in authentic form!
Unharnessed, naked, troops of Moorish horse

Sweep to the charge; more high, the Dacian force,
To hoof and finger mailed; – yet, high or low,
None bleed, and none lie prostrate but the foe;
In every Roman, through all turns of fate,
Is Roman dignity inviolate;
Spirit in him pre-eminent, who guides,
Supports, adorns, and over all presides;
Distinguished only by inherent state
From honoured Instruments that round him wait;
Rise as he may, his grandeur scorns the test
Of outward symbol, nor will deign to rest
On aught by which another is deprest.
– Alas! that One thus disciplined could toil
To enslave whole nations on their native soil;
So emulous of Macedonian fame,
That, when his age was measured with his aim,
He drooped, 'mid else unclouded victories,
And turned his eagles back with deep-drawn sighs.
O weakness of the Great! O folly of the Wise!

Where now the haughty Empire that was spread
With such fond hope? her very speech is dead;
Yet glorious Art the power of Time defies,
And Trajan still, through various enterprise,
Mounts, in this fine illusion, toward the skies:
Still are we present with the imperial Chief,
Nor cease to gaze upon the bold Relief
Till Rome, to silent marble unconfined,
Becomes with all her years a vision of the Mind.

For some visitors to Rome, the ruins of the classical city demonstrated the enduring superiority of Christianity, destined to triumph over the fallen pagan world. This is the dominant note in two Roman sonnets written by Aubrey de Vere (1814–1902), an Irish poet and thinker, and friend of the future Cardinal Manning, who converted to Catholicism in 1851. Whether looking at the Arch of Titus, which commemorates the victories of Titus and Vespasian in the Judaean War, culminating in the sack of Jerusalem in AD 70, or at the Appian Way, the Roman road originally built in 312 BC and later extended as far as Brindisi in southern Italy, de Vere finds in them texts on the historical and moral superiority of Christianity.

The Arch of Titus

Aubrey de Vere

I stood beneath the Arch of Titus long;
On Hebrew forms there sculptured long I pored;
Till fancy, by a distant clarion stung
Woke: and methought there moved that arch toward
A Roman Triumph. Lance and helm and sword
Glittered; white coursers tramped and trumpets rung:
Last came, car-borne a captive horde among
The laurelled Boast of Rome – her destined Lord.
As though by wings of unseen eagles fanned
The Conqueror's cheek when first that Arch he saw
Burned with the flush he strove in vain to quell –
Titus! a loftier arch than thine hath spanned
Rome and the world with empery and law;
Thereof each stone was hewn from Israel!

The Appian Way

Aubrey de Vere

Awe-struck I gazed upon that rock-paved way,
The Appian Road; marmorean witness still
To Rome's resistless stride and fateful Will,
Which mocked at limits, opening out for aye
Divergent paths to one imperial sway –
The Nations verily their parts fulfil;
And War must plough the fields which Law shall till;
Therefore Rome triumphed till the appointed day.
Then from the Catacombs, like waves up-burst
The Host of God, and scaled as in an hour
O'er all the earth the mountain seats of Power.
Gladly in that baptismal flood immersed
The old Empire died to live. Once more on high
It sits; now clothed with immortality.

Two poems by Aldo Palazzeschi, the pen name of Aldo Giurlani (1885–1974), poet and novelist born in Florence and a resident of Rome from the late 1930s, present less doctrinaire accounts of a rather different species of the pleasure of ruins:

November

Aldo Palazzeschi

The young and the old
gather
amidst the warm ruins of Rome,
on which the plane trees let fall

with the sound of paper
their gilded leaves.
The young tell the old
of what they like,
and the old pretend not to hear.

The Palatine

Aldo Palazzeschi

On the soft cushions of time
the body rests
in a torrid summer afternoon.
Thought lacks power to evoke
shades or ghosts,
the eye barely catches
those transparent vapours
that rise from the earth
and which the heat melts into the light.
Drunk dry by the sun
the stones are as white
as anonymous, abandoned tombs,
and the branches tremble lightly
in celestial aspiration.
Through burning abandon
the senses perceive only a scent.
The present stinks
and the future is a vague concept,
the past no longer stinks,
it has a vague scent of dry leaves
the past.

In the introduction to her wonderful book *The Pleasure of Ruins*, first published in 1953, Rose Macaulay speculates on the many different elements which make up our enjoyment of ruins, such as our imaginative recreation of the ruin in its prime, our aesthetic pleasure in its present condition or our exploration of its historical associations; whether perhaps we may take 'a morbid pleasure in decay' or 'a righteous pleasure in retribution (for so often it is the proud and the bad who have fallen)'; whether sometimes we are stirred to 'mystical pleasure in the destruction of all things mortal and the eternity of God' or to a kind of egotistical satisfaction in our own survival. Whatever makes up 'the pleasure of ruins' there are few places more likely to produce such pleasures than Rome.

THE COLOSSEUM

'Unlike any work of human hands'

The Colosseum is one of the most instantly recognisable buildings in the world and has become, effectively, a symbol for Rome itself. It is visited by some three million people each year; many millions more are familiar with its image on film, in picture books or, indeed, on t-shirts and tea towels. The Colosseum was inaugurated in AD80 and was originally known as 'The Ampitheatre' or the 'Hunting Theatre' – it was the Middle Ages which gave it the name of 'Colosseum' (in part, perhaps, because of the colossal statue of Nero that stood near by). It was planned by the Emperor Vespasian, Nero's successor, and was completed by Titus. It was built on the site of the private lake which Nero had created for himself, alongside his Golden House, in the wake of the Great Fire of AD64. It is said to have been opened by a hundred days of bloodshed and spectacle; the poet Martial celebrated both the structure itself and the opening extravaganza of beast-hunts and gladiatorial combat in a series of epigrams.

On Caesar's Amphitheatre

Martial

Egypt, forbear thy Pyramids to praise,
A barb'rous Work up to a Wonder raise;
Let *Babylon* cease th' incessant Toil to prize,
Which made her Walls to such immensness rise;
Nor let th' *Ephesians* boast the curious Art,
Which Wonder to their Temple does impart.

Delos dissemble too the high Renown,
Which did thy Horn-fram'd Altar lately crown;
Caria to vaunt thy Mausoleum spare,
Sumptuous for Cost, and yet for Art more rare,
As not borne up, but pendulous I'th' Air:
All Works to *Caesar*'s Theatre give place,
This Wonder *Fame* above the rest does grace.

Translated by Henry Killigrew

To Caesar, on a Woman's Fighting with a Lion

Martial

'Tis not enough, in this our Martial Age,
That Men, but Women in fierce Combate gage.
Among the noblest Acts *Fame* does resound,
Alcides laid a Lion on the Ground.
Let Fables cease: *Caesar*, at thy Command,
This hath been acted by a Female Hand.

Translated by Henry Killigrew

On Two Gladiators

Martial

Priscus and *Verus*, while with equal Might,
Prolong'd an obstinate and doubtful Fight,
The People, oft, their Mission did desire;
But *Caesar* from the Law would not retire,
Which did the Prize and Victory unite,
Yet gave them what Encouragement he might;
Largess of Meat and Money did bestow,
Which also 'mong the People he did throw.
I'th' end, howe'er, the Strife was equal found,
Both fought alike, and both alike gave ground:
So that the Palm was upon each conferr'd,
Their undecided Valour this deserv'd.
Under no Prince before we e'er did see,
That two should fight, and both should Victors be.

Translated by Henry Killigrew

The Rhinocerite

Martial

Trembling keepers prick the rhinocerite;
Desirous speedy fury to excite.
When expectation began to tire,
The beast's disturbed calmness, fell on fire;
And showed his horns could hoist a bear at ease,
As bulls toss untried mastives when they please.

Translated by Thomas Pecke

The Colosseum continued to be used for fights between gladiators until, at least, the 430s; it was used for the staging of animal hunts for a further hundred years. Whether or not it was ever really flooded to stage mock sea-battles remains a matter of scholarly controversy; Christians were probably martyred there, though no early records exist to prove this. After it had ceased to fulfil its original uses, the real nature of the Colosseum was forgotten and it became the stuff of legend. Some said that Virgil was the architect who designed it! The medieval guide for Christian pilgrims to Rome, *Mirabilia Urbis Romae* (*The Wonders of Rome*), explained the structure as a temple of the Sun, formerly 'covered with a heaven of gilded bronze, in which thunder and lightning and glittering fire were created, and from which rain poured through tubes of silver'. Renaissance scholars evolved a renewed knowledge of its original nature and purposes; Renaissance architects began to admire and learn from it. The physical structure of the building continued to decline and it frequently served as a quarry. In 1594 a glue factory was established within it, and, from the end of the sixteenth century, religious dramas were performed there as well. By the eighteenth century the Colosseum was ready to appeal to the early Romantic fascination with ruins.

The poet and painter John Dyer found in the ruins of the Colosseum a picturesque and melancholy emblem of the ravages of time and human cruelty:

FROM *The Ruins of Rome*

John Dyer

Amid the tow'ry Ruins, huge, supreme,
Th' enormous *Amphitheatre* behold,
Mountainous pile! o'er whose capacious womb
Pours the broad firmament its varied light;
While from the central floor the seats ascend
Round above round, slow-wid'ning, to the verge,
A circuit vast and high: nor less had held
Imperial *Rome*, and her attendant realms,
When drunk with rule she will'd the fierce delight,
And op'd the gloomy caverns, whence out-rush'd,
Before th' innumerable shouting crowd,
The fiery, madded, tyrants of the wilds,
Lions and tigers, wolves and elephants,
And desp'rate men, more fell. Abhorr'd intent!
By frequent converse with familiar death,
To kindle brutal daring apt for war;
To lock the breast, and steel th' obdurate heart,
Amid the piercing cries of sore distress
Impenetrable.

Goethe, in Rome in the winter of 1786–87, recorded his sense of wonder before the Colosseum: 'when one looks at it, everything else seems small; the building is so huge that the soul cannot retain an image of it; in memory it seems smaller than it really is; each time one returns to it, it seems greater than before'. In his account of a visit in February 1787 he celebrates the Colosseum by night, giving voice to what was to become a characteristic Romantic fascination:

For three days in a row we have enjoyed bright and glorious

nights. The Colisseum looked particularly beautiful. It is always closed at night. A hermit lives in a little chapel inside it, and a variety of beggars have made their homes under its crumbling vaults. These last had lit a fire on the floor of the arena and a gentle breeze had driven the smoke from it along the ground, so that the lower parts of the ruin were lost in it; up above the huge walls loomed out of the deeper darkness. We stood and contemplated the scene through the iron gratings, as the moon shone brightly above our heads. Gradually the smoke found its way up and out through every opening, the moon lighting it like a cloud of mist. It was a glorious sight.

Shelley, in a letter to Peacock, wrote ecstatically of the pleasure he took in daily visits to the Colosseum during his short visit to Rome in November 1818:

The Coliseum is unlike any work of human hands I ever saw before. It is of enormous height and circuit, and the arches built of massy stones are piled on one another, and jut into the blue air, shattered into the forms of overhanging rocks. It has been changed by time into the image of an amphitheatre of rocky hills overgrown by the wild olive, the myrtle, and the fig-tree, and threaded by little paths, which wind among its ruined stairs and immeasurable galleries: the copsewood overshadows you as you wander through its labyrinths, and the wild weeds of this climate of flowers bloom under your feet. The arena is covered with grass, and pierces, like the skirts of a natural plain, the chasms of the broken arches around. But a small part of the exterior circumference remains – it is exquisitely light and beautiful; and the effect of the perfection of its architecture, adorned with ranges of Corinthian pilasters, supporting a bold cornice, is such, as to diminish the effect of its greatness. The interior is all ruin. I can scarcely believe that when encrusted with Dorian marble and ornamented by columns of Egyptian granite, its effect could have been so sublime and so impressive as in its present state.

Shelley's emphasis on the vegetation of the Colosseum is entirely understandable. In 1855 the Englishman Richard Deakin published *The Flora of the Colosseum*, listing some 420 species to be found there!

In the nineteenth century it was, above all, the poetry (and personality) of Lord Byron (1788–1824) which did most to shape attitudes towards this central symbol of ancient Rome, of the passage of time, of both the grandeur and the smallness of human endeavour. In Canto IV of *Childe Harold's Pilgrimage* the encounter with the Colosseum prompts – as it surely should – intense self-reflection:

FROM *Childe Harold's Pilgrimage*

Lord Byron

Arches on arches! as it were that Rome,
Collecting the chief trophies of her line,
Would build up all her triumphs in one dome,
Her Coliseum stands; the moonbeams shine
As 'twere its natural torches – for divine
Should be the light which streams here, – to illume
This long-explored but still exhaustless mine
Of Contemplation; and the azure gloom
Of an Italian night, where the deep skies assume

Hues which have words, and speak to ye of Heaven,
Floats o'er this vast and wondrous monument,
And shadows forth its glory. There is given
Unto the things of earth, which Time hath bent,
A Spirit's feeling, and where he hath leant
His hand, but broke his scythe, there is a power
And magic in the ruined battlement,
For which the Palace of the present hour
Must yield its pomp, and wait till Ages are its dower.

Oh, Time! the Beautifier of the dead,
Adorner of the ruin – Comforter
And only Healer when the heart hath bled;
Time! the Corrector where our judgments err,
The test of Truth, Love – sole philosopher,
For all beside are sophists – from thy thrift,
Which never loses though it doth defer –
Time, the Avenger! unto thee I lift
My hands, and eyes, and heart, and crave of thee a gift:

Amidst this wreck, where thou hast made a shrine
And temple more divinely desolate –
Among thy mightier offerings here are mine,
Ruins of years – though few, yet full of fate: –
If thou hast ever seen me too elate,
Hear me not; but if calmly I have borne
Good, and reserved my pride against the hate
Which shall not whelm me, let me not have worn
This iron in my soul in vain – shall *they* not mourn?

Yet more striking – it spawned innumerable imitations – was a passage in Byron's verse drama, *Manfred*. Manfred, the hero-villain of the drama, is a tortured Romantic figure, with Faust-like aspirations and a scorn for most of his fellow men. In the final scene of the play, with death approaching and demons waiting to collect his soul, Manfred remembers an earlier, shaping night in his life:

FROM *Manfred*

Lord Byron

The stars are forth, the moon above the tops
Of the snow-shining mountains, – Beautiful!
I linger yet with Nature, for the Night
Hath been to me a more familiar face
Than that of man; and in her starry shade
Of dim and solitary loveliness,
I learn'd the language of another world.
I do remember me, that in my youth,
When I was wandering, – upon such a night
I stood within the Coliseum's wall,
'Midst the chief relics of almighty Rome;
The trees which grew along the broken arches
Waved dark in the blue midnight, and the stars
Shone through the rents of ruin; from afar
The watch-dog bayed beyond the Tiber; and
More near from out the Cæsars' palace came
The owl's long cry, and, interruptedly,
Of distant sentinels the fitful song
Begun and died upon the gentle wind.
Some cypresses beyond the time-worn breach

Appear'd to skirt the horizon, yet they stood
Within a bowshot. Where the Cæsars dwelt,
And dwell the tuneless birds of night, amidst
A grove which springs through levell'd battlements,
And twines its roots with the imperial hearths,
Ivy usurps the laurel's place of growth;
But the gladiators' bloody Circus stands,
A noble wreck in ruinous perfection,
While Cæsar's chambers, and the Augustan halls,
Grovel on earth in indistinct decay.
And thou didst shine, thou rolling moon, upon
All this, and cast a wide and tender light,
Which soften'd down the hoar austerity
Of rugged desolation, and fill'd up,
As 'twere anew, the gaps of centuries;
Leaving that beautiful which still was so,
And making that which was not, till the place
Became religion, and the heart ran o'er
With silent worship of the great of old, –
The dead but sceptred sovereigns, who still rule
Our spirits from their urns.

Alongside the many lesser writers influenced by Byron's treatment of the Colosseum one more major writer stands out. Edgar Allan Poe made only one attempt at drama. His unfinished play, *Politian*, is set in sixteenth-century Rome. In one scene the eponymous hero, while waiting in the Colosseum to meet his lover Lalage, reflects upon himself and his surroundings:

FROM *Politian*

Edgar Allan Poe

Type of the antique Rome! Rich reliquary
Of lofty contemplation left to Time
By buried centuries of pomp and power!
At length – at length – after so many days
Of weary pilgrimage and burning thirst,
(Thirst for the springs of lore that in thee lie,)
I kneel, an altered and an humble man,
Amid thy shadows, and so drink within
My very soul thy grandeur, gloom, and glory!
She comes not, and the spirit of the place
Oppresses me!
Vastness! and Age! and Memories of Eld!
Silence! and Desolation! and dim Night!
I feel ye now – I feel ye in your strength –
O spells more sure than e'er Judæan king
Taught in the gardens of Gethsemane!
O charms more potent than the rapt Chaldee
Ever drew down from out the quiet stars!
She comes not, and the moon is high in Heaven!
Here, where a hero fell, a column falls!
Here, where the mimic eagle glared in gold,
A midnight vigil holds the swarthy bat!
Here, where the dames of Rome their gilded hair
Waved to the wind, now wave the reed and thistle!
Here, where on golden throne the monarch lolled,
Glides, spectre-like, unto his marble home,
Lit by the wanlight of the hornéd moon,
The swift and silent lizard of the stones!
These crumbling walls – these tottering arcades

These mouldering plinths – these sad and blackened shafts
These vague entablatures: this broken frieze
These shattered cornices, this wreck, this ruin,
These stones, alas! These grey stones are they all
All of the great and the colossal left
By the corrosive hours to Fate and me?
Not all the echoes answer me – not all:
Prophetic sounds and loud arise forever
From us and from all ruin unto the wise,
As from the granite Memnon to the sun.
We rule the hearts of mightiest men: we rule
With a despotic sway all giant minds.
We are not desolate we pallid stones,
Not all our power is gone – not all our Fame
Not all the magic of our high renown
Not all the wonder that encircles us
Not all the mysteries that in us lie
Not all the memories that hang upon
And cling around about us as a garment
Clothing us in a robe of more than glory.

Poe (1809–49), master of the dark narrative, poet and essayist, never visited Italy. His image of the Colosseum was probably derived from Byron (and his imitators) and from the engravings of Piranesi.

THE CHURCHES OF ROME

'All frescoed paradise in adoration'

The churches of Rome are one of the city's great glories, architecturally and artistically. In size they range from the enormous – St Peter's itself, Santa Maria Maggiore or San Paolo fuori le Mura – to the intimate – Santa Prassede or Sant'Antonio dei Portoghesi. In age and architectural style, they range from the early Christian (Santa Sabina) to the Renaissance (Santa Maria della Pace), Baroque (San Carlo alle Quattro Fontane and Sant'Andrea al Quirinale) and beyond.

It is in some of Rome's churches that one is perhaps best able to have a direct experience of the multi-layered nature of Rome's history, of how each period has built on top of earlier periods, the results now wholly integrated, yet as readily distinguishable as the annual growth rings in the trunk of a tree. One church where this is an especially striking phenomenon is San Clemente, not far from the Colosseum. Entering from modern street level the visitor is in a building begun early in the twelfth century and restored in the eighteenth, containing some beautiful twelfth-century mosaics, some handsome tombs and early Renaissance frescoes. Off the south aisle steps lead downwards to lower levels, only rediscovered in the nineteenth century. Going down one level, the visitor enters a very early church, mentioned in the fourth century and restored in the eighth and ninth centuries; again there are early frescoes to be seen, and a Byzantine *Madonna* of the fifth or sixth century. A further set of steps takes the visitor down yet lower, to the remains of a first-century house and to a Temple of Mithras, belonging to the second or third century. At this level one can hear the rushing waters of an underground river, flowing through a drain created in the time of the Roman Republic.

A poem by Robert Gittings (1911–92), biographer of both Keats and Hardy, captures very effectively the experience of visiting San Clemente:

Church of San Clemente, Rome

Robert Gittings

This church then is the world. At first appearing
Bright frescoes to the right, mosaic to the left
All orderly, with sunlight streaming in,
All at life's level; even the small cloister
Dances with living; a lizard like dark lightning
Runs winking over the stones. Return, and still
The church is sun-bathed. The fresh florentine figures
Strengthen their sinews on the wall, the beads
Of gold glaze shimmer in the byzantine arch.
Advance: descend: breath of a different life
Rises immediately from the steps; not death,
Not that sweet hopeless odour, but the lungs
Of another way of breathing, an older pulse
Beating a slower time, like the drip-drop
That speaks untraced behind some hidden wall.
This is below the pavement of the street,
The platform of appearance. This is the place
Worship worked out in the dark, to bury faith
From blind invasion. Wars and miracles
Leap from these walls, an age of ecstasy
And fear, a candle burning low in socket

But straight in pitch. Advance: descend once more
The lowest level, faith at the root of faith.
Bullhead, altar, the stone shelves of the seekers
Huddled, secret, turning towards any sign
That led them through their labyrinthine life
To the far gleam, the distant end of the corridor.
And lower yet? No more: the earth itself,
The mother of streams and men. We shall climb back
The levels, hardly now seeing them, till we stand
Ejected on the unhushed streets of Rome,
With this world's future hanging on our hands.

Santa Cecilia, across the river in Trastevere, dedicated to the patron saint of music, is another church with fascinating Roman remains beneath it – of the saint's own house, in which she was subjected to a lengthy martyrdom (first by being enclosed in the hot room of her own baths and then by an inefficient attempt at beheading). A poem on the church by Peter Riley (born 1940) makes reference to a remarkable sculpture of St Cecilia by Stefano Maderno modelled, it is said, on the saint's body as it appeared, miraculously intact, when exhumed in 1599.

S. Cecilia in Trastevere

Peter Riley

What moves between bright thoughts and finished body?
Music's Idea turns in the clouds and she
Lies on the floor, denied her time, face
Turned away so as not to view her own pain . . .

What moves between is all we live, heavy
And light, banked in winged tiers, that we
Carve our eyes through day to day, kiss
The bed and back to the devastating sight again . . .

I believe in a centre to the wasted life
That is carried before the world and holds love
Through distance and strife to the end of a
Perfect reconciliation however many times
Occluded in failed responses finally standing
Whole and obvious, like an orchard in the rain.

It was in another early church, also dedicated to a female saint, that Robert Browning (1812–89) set one of his finest and most richly ironic dramatic monologues – the exquisite church of Santa Prassede. Browning's worldly Renaissance bishop imagines his grand tomb there (though some of the references in the poem might seem apter to Santa Maria del Popolo). Browning first visited Santa Prassede in October 1844, and the poem was written within a few months of his visit.

The Bishop Orders His Tomb at St Praxed's Church, Rome 15—

Robert Browning

Vanity, saith the Preacher, vanity!
Draw round my bed: is Anselm keeping back?
Nephews – sons mine . . . ah God, I know not! Well –
She, men would have to be your mother once,
Old Gandolf envied me, so fair she was!
What's done is done, and she is dead beside,

Dead long ago, and I am Bishop since,
And as she died so must we die ourselves,
And thence ye may perceive the world's a dream.
Life, how and what is it? As here I lie
In this state-chamber, dying by degrees,
Hours and long hours in the dead night, I ask
'Do I live, am I dead?' Peace, peace seems all.
St Praxed's ever was the church for peace;
And so, about this tomb of mine. I fought
With tooth and nail to save my niche, ye know:
– Old Gandolf came me in, despite my care;
For a shrewd snatch out of the corner south
To grace his carrion with, God curse the same!
Yet still my niche is not so cramp'd but thence
One sees the pulpit o' the epistle-side,
And somewhat of the choir, those silent seats,
And up into the aery dome where live
The angels, and a sunbeam's sure to lurk
And I shall fill my slab of basalt there,
And 'neath my tabernacle take my rest,
With those nine columns round me, two and two,
The odd one at my feet where Anselm stands:
Peachblossom-marble all, the rare, the ripe
As fresh-pour'd red wine of a mighty pulse.
– Old Gandolf with his paltry onion-stone,
Put me where I may look at him! True peach,
Rosy and flawless: how I earn'd the prize!
Draw close: that conflagration of my church
– What then? So much was sav'd if aught were miss'd!
My sons, ye would not be my death? Go dig
The white-grape vineyard where the oil-press stood,
Drop water gently till the surface sinks,

And if ye find . . . Ah God, I know not, I! . . .
Bedded in store of rotten figleaves soft,
And corded up in a tight olive-frail,
Some lump, ah God, of *lapis lazuli*,
Big as a Jew's head cut off at the nape,
Blue as a vein o'er the Madonna's breast . . .
Sons, all have I bequeathed you, villas, all,
That brave Frascati villa with its bath,
So, let the blue lump poise between my knees,
Like God the Father's globe on both his hands
Ye worship in the Jesu Church so gay,
For Gandolf shall not choose but see and burst!
Swift as a weaver's shuttle fleet our years:
Man goeth to the grave, and where is he?
Did I say basalt for my slab, sons? Black –
'Twas ever antique-black I meant! How else
Shall ye contrast my frieze to come beneath?
The bas-relief in bronze ye promis'd me,
Those Pans and Nymphs ye wot of, and perchance
Some tripod, thyrsus, with a vase or so,
The Saviour at his sermon on the mount,
Saint Praxed in a glory, and one Pan
Ready to twitch the Nymph's last garment off,
And Moses with the tables . . . but I know
Ye mark me not! What do they whisper thee,
Child of my bowels, Anselm? Ah, ye hope
To revel down my villas while I gasp
Brick'd o'er with beggar's mouldy travertine
Which Gandolf from his tomb-top chuckles at!
Nay, boys, ye love me – all of jasper, then!
'Tis jasper ye stand pledged to, lest I grieve.
My bath must needs be left behind, alas!

One block, pure green as a pistachio nut,
There's plenty jasper somewhere in the world –
And I shall have Saint Praxed's ear to pray
Horses for ye, and brown Greek manuscripts,
And mistresses with great smooth marbly limbs
– That's if ye carve my epitaph aright,
Choice Latin, picked phrase, Tully's every word,
No gaudy ware like Gandolf's second line –
– Tully, my masters? Ulpian serves his need!
And then how I shall lie through centuries
And hear the blessed mutter of the mass,
And see God made and eaten all day long,
And feel the steady candle-flame, and taste
Good strong thick stupifying incense-smoke!
For as I lie here, hours of the dead night,
Dying in state and by such slow degrees,
I fold my arms as if they clasp'd a crook,
And stretch my feet forth straight as stone can point,
And let the bedclothes, for a mortcloth drop
Into great laps and folds of sculptor's-work:
And as yon tapers dwindle, and strange thoughts
Grow, with a certain humming in my ears,
About the life before I lived this life,
And this life too, Popes, Cardinals and Priests,
St Praxed at his sermon on the mount,
Your tall pale mother with her talking eyes,
And new-found agate urns as fresh as day,
And marble's language, Latin pure, discreet,
– Aha, ELUCESCEBAT, quoth our friend?
No Tully, said I, Ulpian at the best!
Evil and brief hath been my pilgrimage.
All *lapis*, all, sons! Else I give the Pope

My villas: will ye ever eat my heart?
Ever your eyes were as a lizard's quick,
They glitter like your mother's for my soul,
Or to the tripod ye would tie a lynx
That in his struggle throws the thyrsus down,
To comfort me on my entablature
Whereon I am to lie till I must ask
'Do I live, am I dead?' There, leave me, there!
For ye have stabb'd me with ingratitude
To death – ye wish it – God, ye wish it! Stone –
Gritstone, a-crumble! Clammy squares which sweat
As if the corpse they keep were oozing through –
And no more *lapis* to delight the world!
Well, go! I bless ye. Fewer tapers there,
But in a row: and, going, turn your backs
– Ay, like departing altar-ministrants,
And leave me in my church, the church for peace,
That I may watch at leisure if he leers –
Old Gandolf, at me, from his onion-stone,
As still he envied me, so fair she was!

Of Rome's early baroque churches, that of the Gesù
(mentioned in Browning's poem – 'so gay') is one of the most
lavishly decorated, a perfect example of the sumptuous manner
favoured by the Jesuits at the time of its construction around
1570. Spectacular as it is, it can seem more intimidating than
welcoming.

In the Gesù

Charles Tomlinson

All frescoed paradise in adoration,
Saints choir the unanimity each atom feels,
And hearts that cannot rise to the occasion
Are spurned to earth beneath angelic heels.
This is the church triumphant, not so loving
As winged with a resistless certainty:
This is the despotism of the dove,
The empire of love without love's comity.

Charles Tomlinson (born 1927) is not only a fine original poet,
he is also a significant translator of Italian poetry into English,
most notably the work of Attilio Bertolucci (1911–2000).

Of all Rome's frescoed churches it is, of course, the frescoes of
the Sistine Chapel which most forcefully demand the visitor's
attention. Though many later poets have sought to do justice to
the impact of the frescoes, it is Michelangelo (1475–1564) him-
self, whose disturbing and powerful work covers the altar wall and
the barrel vault, who has written most memorably of the sheer
labour and pain involved in the creation of these remarkable
scenes:

To Giovanni da Pistoia

On the Painting of the Sistine Chapel

Michelangelo

I've grown a goitre by dwelling in this den –
    As cats from stagnant streams in Lombardy,
    Or in what other land they hap to be –
    Which drives the belly close beneath the chin:

My beard turns up to heaven; my nape falls in,
  Fixed on my spine: my breast-bone visibly
  Grows like a harp: a rich embroidery
Bedews my face from brush-drops thick and thin.
My loins into my paunch like levers grind:
  My buttock like a crupper bears my weight;
  My feet unguided wander to and fro;
In front my skin grows loose and long; behind,
  By bending it becomes more taut and strait;
  Crosswise I strain me like a Syrian bow:
  Whence false and quaint, I know,
  Must be the fruit of squinting brain and eye;
  For ill can aim the gun that bends awry.
  Come then, Giovanni, try
  To succour my dead pictures and my fame;
  Since foul I fare and painting is my shame.

Translated by John Addington Symonds

Almost without exception the churches of Rome contain
works of art of great interest and beauty. Particularly fine are the
paintings to be found in San Luigi dei Francesi, the French
national church in Rome, not far from Piazza Navona. The most
remarkable works in the church are Caravaggio's three scenes
from the Life of St Matthew. Caravaggio (1571–1610) worked in
Rome between 1592 and 1610. As well as quickly making a
reputation for himself as a painter he led a turbulent life which
saw him constantly in trouble with the authorities – for brawling,
for libelling a fellow painter and, finally, for murder. This last
brought about a flight from Rome. In his long poem *Walks in
Rome* (1987), the English poet F. T. Prince (1912–2003), perhaps
most famous for his second world war poem 'Soldiers Bathing'
(which alludes to a famous cartoon by Michelangelo, known only
from copies), records a visit to the church.

F. T. Prince

Nahman of Bratslav says 'True
faith has no need to grapple
with evidence or research.
Faith comes through silence.'
I see that too,
And enter the French Church

We come here now for the chapel
by Caravaggio.
Christ on the left wall
points a finger to call
Matthew the money-changer –
sitting well-dressed, in no danger

On the right there is rage,
blood, death: in his old age
a naked killer bawling
has cut him down.
A boy wails, and an angel
dives with the martyr's crown

Another angel, behind
the altar between Calling
and Death, indites
the Gospel, and he writes,
looking up as in doubt
of his own mind

At both beginning and end,
grouped as bystanders,
gaudily-dressed idle young

cronies, well-fed parasites
and older panders,
lazily attend

Christ's face is mysterious,
oblique in the strong lights
and shadows. The dense
wild canvases
bully and in the end weary us
with ambiguities

So, feeling himself like us,
back of the murder-scene
Michelangelo Merisi
da Caravaggio
turning, about to go,
looks pale and queasy.

So far as sculpture is concerned, one of the glories of Rome is
the series of works by Gianlorenzo Bernini. As sculptor, architect,
fountain designer – and much else – Bernini (1598–1680)
effectively transformed important aspects of Rome's appearance
during the seventeenth century. Of his many sculptural works in
Rome's churches perhaps none is more astonishing than *The
Ecstasy of St Teresa* in the Cornaro Chapel of Santa Maria della
Vittoria (described by Fanny Kemble as 'a gaudy rich little
church'). In its self-conscious theatricality, in the way in which
the whole design of the chapel controls and directs the viewer's
eye, in its fusion of the visual languages of mysticism and
sexuality – in these and many other ways the Cornaro Chapel
might readily be thought of as the archetypal work of Roman
baroque. Although he spent the last years of his life in Rome, the

English Catholic poet Richard Crashaw (*c.*1612–49) did not see Bernini's representation of St Teresa's Ecstasy – which was not completed until the 1650s. But his own fascination with the figure of the Spanish saint led to his writing, in his 'Hymn to St Teresa', a poem which offers a remarkable verbal equivalent to Bernini's art.

FROM *An Hymn to St Teresa*

Richard Crashaw

Thou art Love's victim; and must die
A death more mystical and high.
Into Love's arms thou shalt let fall
A still-surviving funeral.
His is the Dart must make the Death
Whose stroke shall taste thy hallowed breath;
A Dart thrice dipp'd in that rich flame
Which writes thy Spouse's radiant Name
Upon the roof of Heaven; where aye
It shines, and with a sovereign ray
Beats bright upon the burning faces
Of souls which in that Name's sweet graces
Find everlasting smiles. So rare,
So spiritual, pure, and fair
Must be th' immortal instrument
Upon whose choice point shall be sent
A life so loved; and that there be
Fit executioners for Thee,
The fairest and first-born sons of fire,
Blest Seraphim, shall leave their quire
And turn love's soldiers, upon Thee
To exercise their archery.

O how oft shalt thou complain
Of a sweet and subtle Pain.
Of intolerable Joys;
Of a Death, in which who dies
Loves his death, and dies again.
And would for ever so be slain.
And lives, and dies; and knows not why
To live, but that he thus may never leave to die.
How kindly will thy gentle Heart
Kiss the sweetly-killing Dart!
And close in his embraces keep
Those delicious Wounds, that weep
Balsam to heal themselves with. Thus
When These thy Deaths, so numerous,
Shall all at last die into one,
And melt thy Soul's sweet mansion;
Like a soft lump of incense, hasted
By too hot a fire, and wasted
Into perfuming clouds, so fast
Shalt thou exhale to Heaven at last
In a resolving Sigh, and then
O what? Ask not the Tongues of men.
Angels cannot tell; suffice,
Thy self shall feel thine own full joys
And hold them fast for ever there.
So soon as you first appear,
The moon of maiden stars, thy white
Mistress, attended by such bright
Souls as thy shining self, shall come
And in her first ranks make thee room;
Where 'mongst her snowy family
Immortal welcomes wait for thee.

O what delight, when revealed Life shall stand
And teach thy lips Heaven with His hand;
On which thou now may'st to thy wishes
Heap up thy consecrated kisses.
What joys shall seize thy soul, when She
Bending her blessed eyes on thee
(Those second Smiles of Heaven) shall dart
Her mild rays through thy melting heart!

Angels, thy old friends, there shall greet thee
Glad at their own home now to meet thee.

All thy good works which went before
And waited for thee, at the door,
Shall own thee there; and all in one
Weave a constellation
Of Crowns, with which the King thy Spouse
Shall build up thy triumphant brows.

DEATH, ROME AND THE ENGLISH ROMANTIC POETS

'City of the Soul!'

After the interruption to Italian travel caused by the Napoleonic wars, English visitors were keen to return to Italy, not least to Rome. Amongst the most enthusiastic of visitors were the poets. All of the major Romantic poets – and many lesser figures – made trips to Rome. The tone was set, above all, by Byron. Byron entered Rome on April 29th, 1817; what he saw and felt lies behind much of Canto IV of *Childe Harold*. What he wrote was profoundly influential on later visitors in the nineteenth century (and perhaps beyond).

FROM *Childe Harold's Pilgrimage*

Lord Byron

Oh, Rome! my country! city of the soul!
The orphans of the heart must turn to thee,
Lone mother of dead empires! and control
In their shut breasts their petty misery.
What are our woes and sufferance? Come and see
The cypress, hear the owl, and plod your way
O'er steps of broken thrones and temples, Ye!
Whose agonies are evils of a day –
A world is at our feet as fragile as our clay.

The Niobe of nations! there she stands,
Childless and crownless, in her voiceless woe;

An empty urn within her wither'd hands,
Whose holy dust was scatter'd long ago;
The Scipios' tomb contains no ashes now;
The very sepulchres lie tenantless
Of their heroic dwellers: dost thou flow,
Old Tiber! through a marble wilderness?
Rise, with thy yellow waves, and mantle her distress.

The Goth, the Christian, Time, War, Flood, and Fire,
Have dealt upon the seven-hill'd City's pride;
She saw her glories star by star expire,
And up the steep barbarian monarchs ride,
Where the car climb'd the Capitol; far and wide
Temple and tower went down, nor left a site:
Chaos of ruins! who shall trace the void,
O'er the dim fragments cast a lunar light,
And say, 'here was, or is,' where all is doubly night?

The double night of ages, and of her,
Night's daughter, Ignorance, hath wrapt and wrap
All round us; we but feel our way to err:
The ocean hath his chart, the stars their map,
And Knowledge spreads them on her ample lap;
But Rome is as the desert, where we steer
Stumbling o'er recollections; now we clap
Our hands, and cry 'Eureka!' it is clear –
When but some false mirage of ruin rises near.

Alas! the lofty city! and alas!
The trebly hundred triumphs! and the day
When Brutus made the dagger's edge surpass
The conqueror's sword in bearing fame away!
Alas, for Tully's voice, and Virgil's lay,

And Livy's pictured page! – but these shall be
Her resurrection; all beside – decay.
Alas, for Earth, for never shall we see
That brightness in her eye she bore when Rome was free!

Shelley's excited reaction to the Colosseum and to the Baths of Caracalla – and, indeed, to much else in the city – has been illustrated earlier in this volume. It was in Rome, however, that his son William ('Willmouse') died on June 7th, 1819. He wrote to Peacock the next day:

> Yesterday, after an illness of only a few days, my little William died. There was no hope from the moment of the attack. You will be kind enough to tell all my friends, so that I need not write to them. It is a great exertion to me to write this.

Little William Shelley was buried in the Protestant Cemetery, but some error was made over the gravestone and the exact whereabouts of his body are not known. His father's later associations with Rome were to be death-haunted, one way and another. After an earlier brief visit to Rome he had written (in December 1818) that

> The English burying-place is a green slope near the walls, under the pyramidal tomb of Cestius, and is, I think, the most beautiful and solemn cemetery I ever beheld. To see the sun shining on its bright grass, fresh, when we first visited it, with the autumnal dews, and hear the whispering of the wind among the leaves of the trees which have overgrown the tomb of Cestius, and mark the soil which is stirring in the sun-warm earth, and to mark the tombs, mostly of women and young people who are buried there, one might, if one were to die, desire the sleep they seem to sleep.

Some of these sentiments were to return to Shelley's mind all too soon, on the occasion of John Keats's death in Rome, on February 23rd, 1821. In the preface to his elegy, *Adonais* (1821), he writes that Keats

> was buried in the romantic and lonely cemetery of the Protestants in that city, under the pyramid which is the tomb of Cestius, and the massy walls and towers, now mouldering and desolate, which formed the circuit of ancient Rome. The cemetery is an open space among the ruins, covered in winter with violets and daisies. It might make one in love with death, to think that one should be buried in so sweet a place.

In the course of the poem, Shelley again evokes the atmosphere of the cemetery, to powerful effect:

FROM *Adonais*

Percy Bysshe Shelley

Go thou to Rome, – at once the Paradise,
The grave, the city, and the wilderness;
And where its wrecks like shattered mountains rise,
And flowering weeds, and fragrant copses dress
The bones of Desolation's nakedness
Pass, till the spirit of the spot shall lead
Thy footsteps to a slope of green access
Where, like an infant's smile, over the dead
A light of laughing flowers along the grass is spread;

And gray walls moulder round, on which dull Time
Feeds, like slow fire upon a hoary brand;

And one keen pyramid with wedge sublime,
Pavilioning the dust of him who planned
This refuge for his memory, doth stand
Like flame transformed to marble; and beneath,
A field is spread, on which a newer band
Have pitched in Heaven's smile their camp of death,
Welcoming him we lose with scarce extinguished breath.

Here pause: these graves are all too young as yet
To have outgrown the sorrow which consigned
Its charge to each; and if the seal is set,
Here, on one fountain of a mourning mind,
Break it not thou! too surely shalt thou find
Thine own well full, if thou returnest home,
Of tears and gall. From the world's bitter wind
Seek shelter in the shadow of the tomb.
What Adonais is, why fear we to become?

The One remains, the many change and pass;
Heaven's light forever shines, Earth's shadows fly;
Life, like a dome of many-coloured glass,
Stains the white radiance of Eternity,
Until Death tramples it to fragments. – Die,
If thou wouldst be with that which thou dost seek!
Follow where all is fled! – Rome's azure sky,
Flowers, ruins, statues, music, words, are weak
The glory they transfuse with fitting truth to speak.

In less than a year and a half after Keats, Shelley too was dead.
He drowned in the Bay of Spezzia in July 1822. His friends
cremated his body in a ceremony on the beach on August 16th.
All was consumed, save the heart, rescued by his friend Edward
Trelawny. Eventually, in January of the following year, the heart

and Shelley's ashes were interred in the 'sweet place' he had so admired.

For Thomas Hardy, when he visited Rome in 1887, the tombs of Keats and Shelley far outweighed in importance the grander creation erected in memory of Caius Cestius (praetor and tribune) in the first century BC.

At the Pyramid of Cestius Near the Graves of Shelley and Keats

Thomas Hardy

Who, then, was Cestius,
    And what is he to me?–
Amid thick thoughts and memories multitudinous
    One thought alone brings he.

I can recall no word
    Of anything he did;
For me he is a man who died and was interred
    To leave a pyramid.

Whose purpose was exprest
    Not with its first design,
Nor till, far down in Time, beside it found their rest
    Two countrymen of mine.

Cestius in life, maybe,
    Slew, breathed out threatening;
I know not. This I know: in death all silently
    He does a finer thing,

In beckoning pilgrim feet
  With marble finger high
To where, by shadowy wall and history-haunted street,
  Those matchless singers lie . . .

  –Say, then, he lived and died
  That stones which bear his name
Should mark, through Time, where two immortal Shades abide;
  It is an ample fame.

The cemetery has become a place of pilgrimage for poets and
lovers of poetry. Oscar Wilde visited in 1877, writing sonnets on
the graves of both Keats and Shelley.

The Grave of Keats

Oscar Wilde

Rid of the world's injustice, and his pain
  He rests at last beneath God's veil of blue:
  Taken from life when life and love were new
The youngest of the Martyrs here is lain,
Fair as Sebastian, and as early slain.
  No cypress shades his grave, no funeral yew
  But gentle violets weeping with the dew
Weave on his bones an ever-blossoming chain.
O proudest heart that broke for misery!
  O sweetest lips since those of Mitylene!
  O poet-painter of our English Land!
Thy name was writ in water – it shall stand:
  And tears like mine shall keep thy memory green,
  As Isabella did her Basil-tree.

An interesting sonnet on the grave of Shelley is to be found amongst the poems of Frances Anne Kemble (1809–93), member of the famous theatrical dynasty of the Kembles, who turned to writing after a successful career (which she did not enjoy) as an actress.

To Emilia Lovatelli

*Weeping by Shelley's Grave in
the Protestant Cemetery of Rome*

Fanny Kemble

Lur'd by the Siren's summer song to death,
The Poet fell asleep – and the fine frame,
Shrine of the finer soul, on wings of flame,
Was borne into the air; but underneath
This sacred soil his heart has found a home;
Thy light feet cannot stir its marble sleep,
Nor e'en thy gracious pity wake again
One throbbing pulse of pleasure or of pain.
O noblest daughter of Imperial Rome,
Who by our Poet's grave hast paus'd to weep,
The after-glow of fame warms not his tomb,
Whose laurels only make its gloom more deep;
But the sweet violet wreath his dead heart wears,
Fragrant and fresh, was sown there by thy tears.

I have not been able to identify Emilia Lovatelli. She perhaps belonged to the aristocratic Lovatelli family of Ravenna.

Many later poets have recorded their thoughts and impressions of the cemetery.

In the Protestant Cemetery, Rome

Rome. Sunday morning, 19 February 1978

James Kirkup

*Rome is a good nurse and soon rocks to a quiet
grave those who seek death* MARY SHELLEY

What was it made them choose
this willing exile for their deaths?
Some from the Antipodes; some came from Japan,
even from grim Newcastle upon Tyne –
John Hamilton, and that Isabella
'wife of B. Akenhead Esqre'.

Some died thinking fondly of
the native land now left for ever.
But others gave a sigh of joy to be
released from life, and from the last of England
long grown strange to them.

Here lie Vikings of my own ancestry:
Carsten Hauch, *digteren*,
Edvard Munch, and Axel Munthe,
and all the Germans – young Waiblinger,
Count Keyserling, and Goethe's son.

Under a crumbling gothic tower lies
the grave of Shelley, where at last
the tears flowed through my fingers.
I wiped them on his stone:
They were my only offerings.
Beside him bluff Trelawny,
friend faithful even in death.

In the shadow of the Pyramid of Cestius
the small tablet for William Shelley
'son of Percy and Mary Wolstonecraft'
– died at the age of three.
His father died just three years later:
'Nothing of him that doth fade . . .'

And in the remotest corner, there
where a little opening in the wall
on the Via Calo Cestio allows
the casual passer-by a fleeting glimpse,
the graves of another pair of friends –
Keats and Severn – on this February morning
Carpeted with violets, and sun. He who died
'in the bitterness of his heart,
at the malicious power of his enemies'
is vindicated now – a name not writ in water.

And still they come – the neat rows
of recent graves, recent births, recent burials
all bright with Mediterranean blooms:
a crowded kingdom of the lonely and the lost –
but gladly lost in Italy's immortal earth.
– While in the hectic streets outside the walls
the raving ambulances' steam whistles scream.

Kirkup's poem draws on the wording on the gravestones of the
two great Romantic poets. On that of Keats (on which his name
does not appear) are inscribed the words:

Here lies One
Whose Name was writ in Water

On Shelley's gravestone are quoted three lines from Shakespeare's
The Tempest:

> Nothing of him that doth fade
> But doth suffer a sea-change
> Into something rich and strange

The cemetery remains a beautiful and moving spot – others buried there include Keats's friend Joseph Severn (1793–1879), who accompanied him on his last journey to Rome and later became British Consul there; John Gibson (1790–1866), the English sculptor; John Addington Symonds (1840–93), English man of letters; Gregory Corso (1930–2001), American poet; Antonio Gramsci (1891–1937), Italian communist, and many others.

Keats's last months were spent in lodgings at No.26, Piazza di Spagna. He was able to enjoy the view from the window of these cramped lodgings – the Piazza was then full of lively craft workshops; the Spanish Steps were a meeting place for artists' models seeking employment. In the Piazza the fountain designed by Pietro Bernini, father of the more famous Gianlorenzo, in the shape of a broken boat, offered nocturnal music. At times Keats was well enough to climb the steps and enjoy the view over Rome. It is thoroughly fitting that since 1909 No.26 has served as a museum and library commemorating Keats, Shelley and the other Romantic poets who visited Italy. Is it the result of chance, or of someone's lively wit, that two doors away from the entrance to the Keats-Shelley House (as it is known), there should be a shop trading as 'Byron the Shirtmakers'?

The Keats-Shelley House: Rome 1909

James Rennell Rodd

An old-world house with rusted orange walls,
    Where, in the city's heart, you hear the drip
Of Sabine water plashing as it falls
    Into the marble semblance of a ship:
Its windows open on a giant stair
    Crowned by an obelisk, and higher still
Sun-traced in Rome's gold-radiant air
    The Trinity that names the hill.

Enter the modest portal and ascend
    Those narrow steps where once with labouring breath
He came at even and the journey's end
    Who seeking life was greeted here by death.
The marble stairs are steep, the shade strikes cold
    In midmost summer. Fling the windows wide
And let the Roman sun flood in. Behold
    The place where Adonais died.

Little is changed. The lime-washed walls enclose
    A narrow chamber, with a roof pale blue
Between the rafters, panelled for the rose
    In mock relief that once his wide eyes knew,
Sleeplessly watching till the drooped lids tired:
    A red-tiled floor, and windows whence at times
The lilt of the great city's life inspired
    Suggestion of unwritten rhymes.

And this was all he knew of that great Rome,
    The deathless mother of immortal men,
Dreamed of in visions in his Northern home,

And reached at last, and still beyond his ken:
A window world – blue noon and even's glow,
    The passing pageant of the Spanish Square,
And blown from baskets on the steps below
    The scent of violets in the air.

And here, above yon rampired stairway oft
    Mounting at eve would Shelley pause to gaze
Where the great dome left earth to soar aloft
    A glory centred in a crimson blaze.
And Byron's shadow haunts this Spanish place; –
    Those were his windows, where the master brain
Divined the soul behind the marble face
    And made the dead Rome live again.

And therefore men from either side the sea
    Who speak the same great language, joining hands,
Designed the poet's house of death to be
    A pilgrim shrine for poets of their lands.
So keep, my country, as a holy trust
    The house we tended with our love and care!
Their ashes mix with Rome's immortal dust,
    But in the spirit they are there.

This poem, marking the opening of the Keats-Shelley House, is the work of James Rennell Rodd (1858–1941), an interesting and accomplished man; in his youth, spent in the literary and artistic world of London, he was acquainted with Wilde and Whistler; he entered the diplomatic service, and was British Ambassador in Rome from 1908–19. He was a driving force in the creation of both the Keats-Shelley House and the British School of Archaeology and Arts in Rome. As well as poetry, he published a number of works of classical scholarship. He was created Baron Rennell of Rodd in 1933.

THE POPULAR TRADITION

Pasquino and his heirs

Post-classical Rome has always been home to an often irreverent tradition of popular poetry, especially work written in the Romanesco dialect. A major vehicle for such traditions was provided by the so-called 'speaking statues' of Rome.

Near Piazza Navona, behind the Palazzo Braschi, stands a battered and eroded ancient torso, probably of Menelaus. Since it was placed there at the very beginning of the sixteenth century it has been known as Pasquino (there are competing explanations as to why). It rapidly became the custom to hang satirical epigrams and lampoons upon the statue. The statue gave its name to the literary genre of the pasquinade. Soon it acquired fellows – other statues on which replies, or new poems, appeared. Whole dialogues, by anonymous authors (often necessarily anonymous for their own safety) evolved. The most important of Pasquino's 'companions' were Marforio, a huge statue of a river god, now to be seen in the courtyard of the Palazzo Nuovo in the Piazza del Campidoglio, and Madame Lucrezia, a large classical bust of Isis, now in the Piazza San Marco at the foot of the Corso. When he visted Rome in 1816, the French novelist Stendhal (1783–1842) shrewdly observed that, above all else, the people of Rome wished to be able 'to show their forceful contempt for the powers that control them' and to have a good laugh at their expense. The witticisms displayed on Pasquino and the other speaking statues allowed them to do just that.

Pasquino often had things to say about papal abuses of power. At the death of Urban VIII, pope from 1623 to 1644, Pasquino observed that he had made a better job of looking after his own family (the Barbarini, whose coat of arms included bees) than he had his Christian flock:

> On the tomb of Urban let these words be placed:
> His lambs he fed so badly, his bees so well.

The same pope had earlier ordered the melting down of the bronze ceiling of the Pantheon's portico, for use in Bernini's baldacchino in St Peter's (as well as in some cannons for Castel Sant'Angelo). Pasquino observed contemptuously

> *Quod non fecerunt barbari fecerunt Barberini*
> (What the barbarians didn't do, the Barberini have).

It wasn't only popes that felt the sting of Pasquino's wit. When ex-Queen Christina of Sweden, notorious both for presumption in adopting roles and powers hitherto reserved for men and for her supposed promiscuity, took up residence in Rome, Pasquino was ready to sum her up:

> A Queen without realm,
> A Christian without faith,
> A Woman without shame.

Pasquino continues to be used for the display of satirical verses – more often, now, on the evils and misjudgements of Italian politicians.

Romanesco, the dialect of Rome, has a long and distinguished poetic tradition. One relatively early poet of Romanesco, Giuseppe Berneri (1637–*c*.1700) has been unduly neglected, and even his major poem *Meo Patacca* (1695) is less well known than it should be. A kind of plebeian miniature epic, almost one thousand lines in length, the poem is a fascinating picture of many aspects of life in late seventeenth-century Rome, as lived in the streets and homes of the ordinary man. The poem is set against the background of the Ottoman siege of Vienna in 1683, though much of it is taken up with accounts of public celebrations in Rome after news arrives of the siege having been lifted. Berneri is a witty narrator, who enjoys describing the spectacles of his native city, as in this account of the Piazza Navona:

FROM *Meo Patacca*

Giuseppe Berneri

Deep in thought Meo goes for a stroll
At the pace of an expectant mother,
Soon reaching the open space of Agonale,
That ordinary folk call the Piazza Navona.
In summer the air is fresh without fail
And many enjoy it even when day is done:
A square so beautiful it would be wrong
Not to include it in my song.

In length the place is four hundred strides
As a man might take when out walking;
Or the other way it is about a hundred wide
Give or take a dozen if only strolling.
In more than just corners can be espied
Buildings of a beauty that's outstanding.
While everywhere arranged neatly
Are shops and houses of good quality.

There are fountains either end of the square
Which it is not over-the-top to suggest
Are justly praised by visitors there
Who've travelled both East and West:
Their basins are spacious, curvilinear –

A shape that is oval at best;
And along each rim the eye detects
Carved corners of beauty without defects.

Similar are those fountains' basins
Made of marble, but there is a difference:
Four grotesque faces fashioned by stone-masons
Appear with effect along the lower rim of one;
While farther back are fitted funny Tritons
Arranged in such a way as to make sense
That, although spread with irregularity,
They yet act like an ensemble of hilarity.

Bang in the middle of the basin, upright
Is a statue posing on a travertine base:
A bit of a yob, seeming not very bright
From the expression on his face.
And by his left side, first his right
Then left hand grip a creature like a porpoise
By its tail, while his look changes to fear
As the moment he may fall gets near.

And between the thighs of this stone man
The great fish, twisting and turning behind,
Thrusts out its head like a watering-can,
Sending from its mouth a cascade all around;
And this without mixing with deluge from
The faces the lower rim has nearly drowned:
And thus is one fountain so complex there,
While the other is simple, unadorned and bare.

Even so, both fountains are richly beautiful,
Though neither has much in common

With the fountain facing them and central
To this square that acts as their home.
To compare them with the one in the middle
Makes each seem a very small fountain alone,
Despite the fact that one who knows his sculpture
Considers them as equalling the best works for sure.

As a basin its shape is perfection:
In the outer part a layer of bricks
Forms a platform that needs no correction
Save for a slight incline, one of those builder's tricks,
That should water overflow its direction
It would be drained of all errant slicks;
While around are set small pillars and
A railing where one may sit or stand.

A heap of stones placed in the fountain
Almost form a great rock with a hole
Running side to side of this little mountain
With further, lesser gaps throughout the whole.
On some of the stones that the waterflow detain
Weeds are sprouting out of control;
And the gaze is fooled, and the mind too
If it did not guess this rock unreal, untrue.

The great heap looks close to falling:
Astonishing it does not collapse
As more than one flaw looks appalling
And the stones have multiple cracks.
Indeed, the ingenuous visitor stalling,
Who before it suddenly stops,
Thinks, 'What a fine work's this construction!
Yet may it not fall soon to destruction?'

The ill-informed are unable to appreciate
The ingenuity of such a piece of architecture.
Staring at the thing they consternate
And apprehend that it will crash for sure,
Being unable to understand or calculate
That often it is art that deceives nature,
As this by its wonderful design surely does:
What seems random creation is pure genius.

Additionally, a like number of figures
Stand at four corners, one to each side;
Figures elegantly seated – figures
Reclining that only art could have made.
They symbolize rivers, ancient mapped rivers,
Rivers drawn from far and wide:
The Nile, the Ganges, the Danube, and a
New World river called the Rio de la Plata.

One figure is astonished, in ecstasy;
Another facing is likewise amazed
While holding a crest of the nobility,
The family Pamphilj, their titles upraised:
So that my Muse curtsies in praise,
Yet raises her eyebrows with irony
At having to pay respect to the Dove,
Bird holding the olive twig of peace and love.

Though beneath this rock with its hollow
That does not seem capable of sustaining
The slightest of weights (let us allow
It is a ruin beyond maintaining),
An obelisk rests on it even so –
Called 'the Spire' by common mis-naming –

A great obelisk, steady and ready to endure,
With no intention of falling you may be sure.

To that Spire two rivers turn towards,
Bewildered and suppliant with hands upraised
Not seeking or expecting any rewards,
But in a state of wonder, truly amazed.
From the four seated figures water flows outwards;
From the cracks too, and fills the basin like a crazed
Pouring downwards in ever greater streams,
Spreading outwards its gleeful gleams.

Like a little duck in swamp or lake,
A dolphin wallows in a similar way –
And another fish too shares the watery intake
From the great basin filled each day
Before the overflow below is piped away
Down the drain in the centre of the square:
And a sculpted horse may be seen
Raising its front legs in another scene.

From a shadowy den depicted there as well
A thirsty lion emerges onto the stones,
Balancing there and holding quite still:
Its shoulders flexing neck, sinews and bones,
And parched tongue protruding but quite unable
To reach the water level, try as it will:
It stretches and stretches but can scarcely
Touch the water, remaining forever thirsty.

A palm tree leans against the big rock,
Its trunk all rough and scaly;
And, beneath, one sees with a bit of a shock,
A half-curled crocodile in a corner dimly.

But, finally, having depicted the lot
Of this art of water and rock,
It only remains to name (it is not me)
The author of this work: *Bernini*.

Translated by William Oxley

Berneri's eponymous hero gives his name to a lively and popular restaurant in Trastevere. Elsewhere in Trastevere – in Piazza Gioacchino Belli – one can see a delightful statue of a later, and somewhat better known Romanesco poet, Giuseppe Gioacchino Belli (1791–1863). Belli was in many ways a rather conservative figure, and most of his work was written in the conventional Italian of his day. But in the 1830s (mostly between 1831 and 1836) he wrote some two thousand sonnets in Romanesco. His aim, he declared, was 'to set down the words of the Roman just as they issue from his mouth, without ornament or alteration, without inversions or poetical licenses'. Papal corruption, poverty, prostitution and much else provided the subject matter of Belli's Romanesco sonnets – almost none of which were published during his lifetime. Most are governed by a kind of amused observation of the absurdities of human behaviour, as evidenced by life in Rome.

The Funeral of Pope Leo XII

G. G. Belli

Last night the late great Pope went cruising by
Pasquino's corner, right in front of us,
head nodding on a bed of fluffiness
just like an angel kipping on the sly;

and then the muted buglers came on down,
and drummers drumming with a muffled din,
and mules to haul the mighty baldaquin,
and then the papal keys and papal crown;

friars and priests, and next a clapped-out gun,
and grooms who held aloft their flaming tapers,
and then those bloody guardsmen on display.

The bells of all the churches tolled as one
the moment that the corpse went on its way . . .
This country has such entertaining capers!

Translated by Mike Stocks

Belli's poem is dated November 26th, 1831. Leo XII actually
died on February 10th, 1829.

The Ingenuity of Man

G. G. Belli

At evensong on Friday last but one
I met with Margaret in the street outside,
went running up the Corso arms held wide:
'I'm gagging for it Mags, let's get it on!'

'But where?' she said, so quick as quick can be
I fixed her with my hat and coat to wear
and both of us skedaddled out of there
and in the Garavita sneakily.

Inside it's dungeon-dark, and any lights
are dimmed down further for the penance rites,
after the rosary is said aloud.

Well then, in a confessional we set to,
and got all hot and bothered, as you do,
just underneath *The Station of the Shroud*.

Translated by Mike Stocks, 2007

Dated December 18th, 1832, Belli's poem sets its narrative of human ingenuity in the service of lust in the church of Sant' Ingrazio, on the Via del Caravita ('Garavita' in Romanesco) between the Corso and the Pantheon. The adventure apparently reaches its climax in a confessional beneath a representation of 'The Station of the Shroud', the last of the fourteen Stations of the Cross, the entombment of Christ. Roman irreverence reaches something of an apogee in poems such as this.

MODERN ROME

'Stupendous, miserable city'

To wander the streets of contemporary Rome – or, indeed, to work there – is to encounter juxtapositions of past and present constantly, to find oneself somehow lost in time, outside the merely temporal nature of one's body, silently part of some larger harmony.

O Rome

Thomas Kinsella

O Rome thou art, at coffee break, O Rome
Thou also art a town of staring clerks,
Staring the azure window at mid-morning,
Commemorating something in a daze.

Dissociated from the flesh, upright
In attitude, they sit like organ pipes
Stale vapours of antiquity sigh through.
Each simple, all in stock-still harmony.

It is too easy to idealise Rome, to lose sight of the reality in a dream, in the Rome of the Imagination. Amongst modern Italian poets no one has kept a tighter grip on the realities (whilst also responding to a particular version of what one might loosely call the 'magic' of Rome) than Pier Paolo Pasolini (1922–75). Pasolini, of course, was far more than just a poet – he was novelist and film director, philosopher and critic – and much else too. Controversial in terms of his political, sexual, social and religious attitudes, Pasolini articulated a marginal Rome, examined areas of society and thought from which the more conventional preferred to avert their eyes. A complex, even contradictory, man and thinker, one of Pasolini's finest achievements as a poet is his 'Le ceneri di Gramsci' (The Ashes of Gramsci), a poem written in 1954, an extended meditation which takes as its starting point the grave of Antonio Gramsci, Marxist thinker and politician. Pasolini's startling – and beautiful – poem marvellously puts forward the claims of the poor and desperate of post-war Rome. Its opening evokes place, time and attitude compellingly:

FROM *Gramsci's Ashes*

Pier Paolo Pasolini

There's nothing May-like in this toxic air
which further darkens or with blazing light
blinds the dark garden of the foreigner
and nothing May-like in the soapy cloud
casting its veil on the vast amphitheatre
of yellow attics ranged beside the mud
of the Tiber and among the purple pines
of Rome. Autumnal spring spreads mortal peace,
though disabused like all our destinies,
over the ancient stones, exhausted now,
and finished ruins where the strong
ingenuous impulse to start life anew
crumbled; and now silence, hot but hard,
where a motorbike whines off into the blue.
A boy in that far spring when even wrong
was at least vigorous, that Italian spring
our parents knew, vital with earth and song

and so much less distracted, when the place
united in fanaticism, you drew
already, brother, with your skinny paw
the ideal society which might come to birth
in silence, a society not for us
since we lie dead with you in the wet earth.

There remains now for you only a long
rest here in the 'non-Catholic' cemetery,
a last internment though this time among
boredom and privilege; and the only cries
you hear are a few final hammer-blows
from an industrial neighbourhood which rise
in the evening over wretched roofs, a grey
rubble of tin cans and scrap metal where
with a fierce song a boy rounds out his day
grinning, while the last rain falls everywhere.

Translated by Derek Mahon

Elsewhere in Pasolini's work, the imaginative record of his Roman wanderings has a unique honesty and range of sympathy, as in this passage on Trastevere:

FROM *The Tears of the Excavator*

Pier Paolo Pasolini

Stupendous, miserable
city, you made me

experience that unknown
life, you made me discover
what the world was for everyone.

A moon dying in the silence that she
feeds goes white amid violent glowing,
which, miserably, on the silent earth,

with its beautiful avenues and old
lanes, dazzles them without shedding
light, while a few hot cloud masses

reflect them to her, above, all over the world.
It's the most beautiful night of summer.
Trastevere, which smells of emptied

taverns and straw from old
stables, isn't asleep yet.
Its dark corners and peaceful walls

resound with enchanted sounds.
Men and boys are strolling home
– beneath abandoned garlands of lights –

toward their alleyways clogged by
darkness and garbage, with that slow pace
which invaded the depths of my soul

when I truly loved, when
I truly wanted to understand.
And, as then, they disappear, singing.

Translated by Norman MacAfee and
Luciano Martinengo

Late in his life, Cesare Pavese (1908–50), novelist, translator, critic and poet, wrote a series of radiant love lyrics. The following poem he dated '28th March, 1950'. Pavese committed suicide on August 27th in the same year.

I Will Pass through Piazza di Spagna

Cesare Pavese

It will be a clear sky.
The streets will open
onto a hill of pine and stone.
The commotion in the streets
won't change that still air.
The flowers splashed
with colour round the fountain
will peep out like women
amused. The steps
the terraces the swallows
will sing in the sun.
That street will open up,
the stones will sing,
the heart will beat, leaping
like water in fountains –
this will be the voice
that ascends your steps.
The windows will know
the smell of stone and morning
air. A door will open.
The commotion of the streets
will be the commotion of the heart
in the bewildered light.

It will be you – still and clear.

28th March, 1950

A central pleasure of contemporary Roman life is in the enjoyment of its restaurants and cafés. Not, of course, that this is a pleasure unique to the present. The cafés of Rome have long been cultural and social centres of great significance. One of the finest and most important is the Caffè Greco, on Via Condotti, between the Corso and Piazza di Spagna. Established in 1760, its patrons over the years have included Goethe, Byron, Liszt, Berlioz, Stendhal, Wagner and D'Annunzio. It was in the Caffè Greco that, in 1861, William Wetmore Story, the American sculptor, introduced Hans Christian Andersen to Elizabeth Barrett Browning! A later meeting is recorded by Czeslaw Milosz (1911–2004), Polish poet of Lithuanian family:

Caffè Greco

Rome, 1986

Czeslaw Milosz

In the eighties of the twentieth century, in Rome, via
    Condotti
We were sitting with Turowicz in the Caffè Greco
And I spoke in, more or less, these words:

– We have seen much, comprehended much.
States were falling, countries passed away.
Chimeras of the human mind besieged us
And made people perish or sink into slavery.
The swallows of Rome wake me up at dawn
And I feel then transitoriness, the lightness
Of detaching myself. Who I am, who I was
Is not so important. Because others,

Noble-minded, great, sustain me
Anytime I think of them. Of the hierarchy of beings.
Those who gave testimony to their faith,
Whose names are erased or trampled to the ground
Continue to visit us. From them we take the measure,
Aesthetic, I should say, of works, expectations, designs.
By what can literature redeem itself
If not by a melopoeia of praise, a hymn
Even unintended? And you have my admiration,
For you accomplished more than did my companions
Who once sat here, the proud geniuses.
Why they grieved over their lack of virtue,
Why they felt such pangs of conscience, I now understand.
With age and with the waning of this age
One learns to value wisdom, and simple goodness.
Maritain[7] whom we used to read long ago
Would have reason to be glad. And for me: amazement
That the city of Rome stands, that we meet again,
That I still exist for a moment, myself and the swallows.

Translated by Milosz and Robert Hass

Jerzy Turowicz (1912–99) was an influential lay-Catholic
commentator during and after the Communist rule of Poland.

---

7   Jacques Maritain (1882–1973), French philosopher.

The English poet and novelist Barry Cole (born 1936) wryly observes life in two less grand establishments, both in the lively area around Stazione Termini, Rome's main railway station (the trattoria Dell'Omo is in Via Vicenza, too).

In Bar Rossi, Via Vicenza

Barry Cole

Early morning's best, a dozen
teenage girls mill for coffee, perch
at nearby tables. They're like a
late dawn chorus (metaphors and
similes hang in the air's twigs).
Eyes agog, my notebook is shut.

At Dell'Omo

Barry Cole

Al vostro servizio del
1950. In the history
of a life perhaps, but not Rome.
Gino, almost venerable
flicks a serviette at breadcrumbs
flecking the linen tablecloth.

Less handsome than homely
this trattoria, so near yet
far from the Termini station.
It has taken us a dozen years
to earn his smile of greeting;
his heir is close upon his heels.

The traditional Roman pleasure of people-watching can be very successfully conducted either from a seat outside a café or, indeed, from a seat inside.

Rome: in the Café

James Laughlin

She comes at eleven every morning
to meet a man who makes her cry

they sit at a table in the back row
talking very earnestly and soon

she begins to cry   he holds her
hand and reasons with her & she

tries to smile when he leaves
her   then she cries again and

orders a brandy and gulps it
down   then she mak es her face

new and goes home   yes I think
that she knows that I come just

to watch her & wait for the day
when he does not come at all.

James Laughlin (1914–97) was a writer and publisher/editor of New Directions – the publishing house which published works by, amongst others, Ezra Pound, Vladimir Nabokov, William Carlos Williams, Dylan Thomas and Jorge Luis Borges.

Such minor pleasures as people-watching should not blind us to the dark side of Rome. A history of Roman violence and brutality – Romulus's murder of Remus having set an example all too frequently imitated – would be a very sizeable volume (if one, indeed, were sufficient). Amongst recent acts of Roman violence, one of immense literary significance stands out. On November 2nd, 1975, Pasolini was savagely murdered on the beach at Ostia, Rome's seaside resort. He was run over several times by his own car. Even now, the murder has not been explained in a fully satisfactory fashion.

Ecce Homo
Pier Pasolini: Report on an Inquest

James Kirkup

When the body was found,
Pasolini was lying full-length,
face-down, one bleeding arm stretched out,
the other twisted underneath him.
His cheeks, so hollow in life,
puffed out by grotesque swellings.
His hair, sticky with blood, hung over
his scratched and torn forehead.
His face, punched out of shape,
was black with bruises, scored by knife wounds.
The hands, too, were pierced, with splintered palms,
and, like the racked arms, red with blood.
The fingers of his left hand
had been smashed, slashed.
The left jaw was fractured.
The nose flattened
and wrenched to the right.
The right ear half cut off,

the one on the left
hanging loosely, torn away.
There were stab wounds on the shoulders,
the thorax, the loins, with marks
made by the tyre treads of his car wheels
under which he had been crushed to death.
A horrible laceration
between the throat and the nape.
On the testicles,
Extensive, deep bruising.
Ten fractured ribs, fractured sternum.
The liver ruptured in two places.
The heart burst.

From *Corriere della Sera*, November 2nd, 1977

Some of the best of modern English poems on Rome have been the work of Peter Porter, born in Australia in 1929 but resident in England since 1951. One of the finest confronts those very questions which life in Rome, despite her beauty, seems fated to pose – questions of death and the human condition.

Crossing the Tiber Island

Peter Porter

This is God's Circus Maximus –
a fledgling sparrow slides from pavement to flutter
and miraculously avoiding Rome's traffic
lives to skid by panic wing-power
into the opposite gutter
and crouches there dynastically.
This is no true contest,
Rome has turned its thumbs down

125

on yet another creature, the Tiber Island
shakes with heat and gravity.
Are not two sparrows sold for a farthing?
They would not fetch so much today
in this expensive city. Gods come here to die
and now a grist of shit and faith
covers Romulus's mound to seventy feet.
We cup our blood for dreams to drink,
thinking we have so many good and evil acts
to chorus us, stones of faith outstaring nerves
beside trompe l'œil ceilings where
bath night fronts a deathless Pantheon.
Each human mind is Rome ruled by a mad
and metaphorical Emperor, or Pope
praised for piddling fountains
and passing barley-sugar baldachinos.
Stepping from the hotel's air-conditioning
you become a city sight-seeing in a city,
your history is just as marvellous as Rome's,
your catacombs the haunt of pilgrims
from Hyperborean archipelagos,
new worlds pillaged of their optimism
to gild a lavishly despairing faith,
the Tiber Island is the food you eat,
the cows ten times your weight, the little
prawns inside their carapace, and lettuce
dressed to ease Christ's vegetarian pain.
The sparrow in the dust
knows neither Pontifex nor Aesculapius
but twitches on its bed of wings
terrorizing Heaven and whichever
deity could meet its dying eye.

LEAVING THE CITY

Arrivederci Roma

In the third of Juvenal's *Satires* the poet meets an old friend called Umbricius who has decided to leave Rome, out of disgust and disappointment, and to move to the isolated spot of Cumae, 'home' of the Cumaen Sibyl and the place where Daedalus ended his flight. The opening passages of the poem are full of vivid topographical details – the falling houses and fires of urban Rome, the 'conduit-gate' (i.e. the Porta Capena, now known as the Porta S. Sebastiana) – and full of Umbricius's complaints against the dishonesty and hypocrisy which, he says, is now the way to get on in Rome:

> Grieved tho' I am, an ancient friend to lose,
> I like the solitary seat he chose:
> In quiet *Cumae* fixing his repose:
> Where, far from noisy *Rome* secure he lives,
> And one more citizen to *Sybil* gives.
> The road to *Bajae,* and that soft recess
> Which all the Gods with all their bounty bless.
> Tho' I in *Prochyta* with greater ease
> Could live, than in a street of palaces.
> What scene so desert, or so full of Fright,
> As tow'ring houses tumbling in the night,
> And *Rome* on fire beheld by its own blazing light?
> But worse than all, the clatt'ring Tiles; and worse
> Than thousand padders, is the poet's curse.
> Rogues that in dog-days cannot rhyme forbear;
> But without mercy read, and make you hear.

Now while my friend just ready to depart,
Was packing all his goods in one poor cart;
He stopped a little at the conduit-gate,
Where *Numa* modelled once the *Roman* State,
In mighty councils with his nymphs retired:
Though now the sacred shades and founts are hir'd
By banish'd Jews, who their whole wealth can lay
In small basket, on a wisp of hay.
Yet such our avarice is, that every tree
Pays for his head; not sleep itself is free:
Nor place, nor persons now are sacred held
From their own grove the Muses are expelled.
Into this lonely vale our steps we bend,
I and my sullen discontented friend:
The marble caves, and aqueducts we view;
But how adult'rate now, and different from the true!
How much more beauteous had the fountain been
Embellished with her first created green,
Where crystal streams through living turf had run
Contented with an urn of native stone!
Then thus *Umbricius,* (with an angry frown,
And looking back on this degen'rate town,)

    'Since noble arts in *Rome* have no support,
And ragged virtue not a friend at court,
No profit rises from th'ungrateful stage,
My poverty increasing with my age,
'Tis time to give my just disdain a vent,
And, cursing, leave so base a government.
Where *Dedalus* his borrowed wings laid by,
To that obscure Retreat I choose to fly:
While yet few furrows on my face are seen,
While I walk upright, and old age is green,

And *Lachesis* has somewhat left to spin.
Now, now 'tis time to quit this cursed place;
And hide from villains my too honest face:
Here let *Arturius* live, and such as he;
Such manners will with such a town agree.
Knaves who in full assemblies have the knack
Of turning truth to lies, and white to black:
Can hire large houses, and oppress the poor
By farmed excise; can cleanse the common shore
And rent the fishery; can bear the dead;
And teach their eyes dissembled tears to shed:
All this for gain; for gain they sell their very head.
These fellows (see what Fortune's pow'r can do)
Were once the minstrels of a country show:
Followed the prizes through each paltry town,
By trumpet-cheeks, and bloated faces known.
But now, grown rich, on drunken holidays,
At their own costs exhibit public plays;
Where influenced by the rabble's bloody will,
With thumbs bent back, they popularly kill.
From thence returned, their sordid avarice rakes
In excrements again, and hires the jakes.
Why hire they not the town, not ev'ry thing,
Since such as they have Fortune in a string?
Who, for her pleasure, can her fools advance;
And toss 'em topmost on the wheel of chance.
What's *Rome* to me, what business have I there,
I who can neither lie nor falsely swear?
Nor praise my patron's undeserving rhymes,
Nor yet comply with him, nor with his times;
Unskilled in schemes by planets to foreshow
Like canting rascals, how the wars will go:

I neither will, nor can prognosticate
To the young gaping heir, his father's fate:
Nor in the entrails of a Toad have pried,
Nor carried bawdy presents to a bride:
For want of these town virtues, thus, alone,
I go conducted on my way by none:
Like a dead member from the body rent;
Maimed and unuseful to the government.
Who now is loved, but he who loves the times,
Conscious of close intrigues and dipped in crimes:
Lab'ring with secrets which his bosom burn,
Yet never must to public light return;
They get reward alone who can betray:
For keeping honest counsels none will pay.

Translated by John Dryden, 1693

Juvenal tells us that he too would prefer to leave Rome, would prefer life on Prochyta (a desolate and barren island) to life in 'a street of palaces'. Details of Juvenal's life (*c.* AD 50–*c.* 127) are hard to come by and he may have had a spell of exile from Rome – but not, one suspects, voluntarily; like most satirists he needed the very thing, the very place, of which his poetry expressed such strong disapproval.

In the case of Ovid and *his* exile, we have some information, but not as much as we might like. In the winter of AD 8 Ovid was banished from Rome by the Emperor Augustus. Ovid's own writings offer two accounts of why he was banished – because his poem *The Art of Love* was judged immoral and/or because of some unexplained 'indiscretion' or 'error', which seems (according to Ovid) to have involved his being a witness of criminal activity by others. Whatever the precise reasons, he was banished to Tomis (now Constanta in Romania) on the shores of the Black Sea. He continued to write from his exile, and amongst the poems there is a moving account of the very night of his departure from Rome:

Nagging reminders: the black ghost-melancholy vision
   of my final night in Rome,
the night I abandoned so much I dearly treasured –
   to think of it, even now, starts tears.

That day was near dawning on which, by Caesar's fiat,
   I must leave the frontiers of Italy behind.
I'd lacked time – and inclination – to get things ready,
   long procrastination had numbed my will:
Too listless to bother with choosing slaves, attendants,
   the wardrobe, the outfit an exile needs,
I was dazed, like someone struck by Jove's own lightning
   (had I not been?), who survives, yet remains unsure
whether he's dead or alive. Sheer force of grief unclouded
   my mind in the end. When my poor wits revived
I had one last word with my friends before departure –
   those few friends, out of many, who stood firm.
My wife, my lover, embraced me, outwept my weeping,
   her undeserving cheeks
rivered with tears. Far away in north Africa, my daughter
   could know nothing of my fate. From every side,
wherever you looked, came the sounds of grief
                              and lamentation,
   just like a noisy funeral. The whole house
mourned at my obsequies – men, women, even children,
   every nook and corner had its tears.
If I may gloss the trite with a lofty comparison,
   such was Troy's state when it fell.

131

By now all was still, no voices, no barking watchdogs,
    just the Moon on her course aloft in the night sky.
Gazing at her, and the Capitol – clear now by moonlight,
    close (but what use?) to my home,
I cried: 'All you powers who dwell in that neighbour citadel,
    you temples, never more to be viewed
by me, you high gods of Rome, whom I must now abandon,
    accept my salutation for all time!
And although I assume my shield so late, after being wounded,
    yet free this my exile from the burden of hate,
and tell that *heavenly man* what error beguiled me, let him
    not think my remissness a crime – so that what *you* know
may likewise be discerned by the author of my expulsion:
    with godhead appeased, I cannot be downcast.'
Such my prayer to the powers above; my wife's were countless,
    sobs choked each half-spoken word;
she flung herself down, hair loose, before our familial
    shrine, touched the dead-cold hearth with trembling lips,
poured out torrential appeals on behalf of the husband
    she mourned in vain. Our little household gods
turned a deaf ear, the Bear wheeled round the Pole Star,
    and ebbing dark left no room
for further delay. What to do? Seductive love of country
    held me back – but this night was decreed my last,
tomorrow came exile. The times friends said 'Hurry!'
                     'Why?' I'd ask them,
  'Think to what place you're rushing me – and from where!'
The times I lied, swearing I'd set up an appropriate
    Departure time for my journey! Thrice I tripped
on the threshold, thrice turned back, dragging lethargic
    feet, their pace matched to my mood.

Often I'd make my farewells – and then go on talking,
　　kiss everyone goodbye all over again,
unconsciously repeat identical instructions, eyes yearning
　　back to my loved ones. In the end –
'Why make haste?' I exclaimed, 'it's Scythia I'm being sent to,
　　it's Rome I must leave: each one a prime excuse
for postponement: my living wife is denied her living
　　husband for evermore: dear family, home,
loyal and much-loved companions, bonded in brotherhood
　　that Theseus might have envied – all
now lost to me. This may well be my final chance to
　　　　　　　　　　　　　　　　embrace them –
　　let me make the most of one last extra hour.'
With that I broke off, leaving my speech unfinished,
　　and hugged all my dear ones in turn –
but while I'd been speaking, and amid their tears, the morning
　　star (so baneful to me) had risen high
and bright in the heavens. I felt myself ripped asunder
　　as though I'd lost a limb; a part of me
seemed wrenched from my body. So Mettus must have suffered
　　when the horses avenging his treachery tore him in two.
Now my family's clamorous weeping reached its climax,
　　sad hands beat naked breasts,
and my wife clung to me at the moment of my departure,
　　making one last agonized tearful plea:
'They can't tear you from me – together', she cried,
　　　　　　　　　　　　　　　　'we'll voyage
　　together, I'll follow you into exile, be
an exile's wife. Mine, too, the journey; that frontier station
　　has room for me as well: I'll make little weight
on the vessel of banishment! While your expulsion's caused by
　　the wrath of Caesar, mine springs from loyal love:

133

this love will be Caesar for me.' Her argument was familiar,
    she'd tried it before and she only gave it up –
still reluctant – on practical grounds. So I made my exit,
    dirty, unshaven, hair anyhow – like a corpse
minus the funeral. Grief-stricken, mind whirling-black,
                      she fainted
    (they tell me), fell down half-dead,
and when she came round, hair foul with dust, and staggered
    back to her feet from the cold floor,
wept now for herself, and now for hearth and household
    bereft of their lord, cried her lost husband's name
again and again, groaning as though she'd witnessed
    her daughter's corpse, or mine,
on the high-stack'd pyre; longed to die, to expunge by dying
    all awareness – yet through her regard for me
could not perish. Let her live, then, ever to succour
    Ovid's exile, since this is what fate has willed.

Translated by Peter Green

For most modern visitors, leaving Rome is unlikely to be so painful. But for many, certainly, there is a sense of loss, perhaps a sense of frustration – grounded in the awareness that *Roma, non basta una vita* (*Rome, A Lifetime is not Enough*), to quote the title of a 1962 book by the Italian writer and journalist Silvio Negro. Most will, surely, want to return – again and again.

Since at least the nineteenth century, the Trevi Fountain, Niccolo Salvi's glorious baroque creation of the previous century, has featured in rituals designed to guarantee the visitor's return to Rome. In the nineteenth century it was said that those who drank from the fountain would be sure to return. It later became urban folklore that if you threw a coin over your shoulder into the fountain you could be certain of returning; throw two and you would fall in love with an Italian; a third and you would marry him or her. A more cynical contemporary Roman version has it that two coins will ensure that a marriage will happen soon, while three coins bring about a divorce!

Fold

Sharon Morris

My heart of stone runs like carved rock –
horses, bearded gods, the flowing
vine of the Trevi fountain.
Folds of the Baroque, striated
as though compressed
in the intense vision of Nicola Salvi,

giant tritons, one blowing on a conch-shell
like a wild trumpet, lead the horses
that pull Neptune's chariot,
caught in mid-gallop their hooves
thrashing up jets of spray,
this tiny piazza fills with the roar of water.

But it's the small details that fascinate us –
the release of grapes, leaves, tendrils
that branch like vein under our skin.
With all the other tourists we throw a coin
Over our shoulder into the fountain
as a promise –

Sharon Morris was born in Wales and currently teaches at the Slade School of Art. Her first collection, *False Spring* (2007), from which this poem is taken, contains a sequence of fine poems on Rome.

It is perhaps fitting that the Trevi Fountain should have become associated with modern folk traditions, since the cinema has made it one of the modern icons of Rome – notably *Roman Holiday* (1953), *Three Coins in the Fountain* (1954) and *La Dolce Vita* (1960). The scene in this last film in which Anita Ekberg (followed by Marcello Mastroianni) immersed herself in the Trevi Fountain has become part of the language now used for the representation of Rome, so much so that Cecilia Bartoli's 2005 CD, *Opera Proibita*, made up of arias written as part of oratorios performed in Rome in the first decade of the eighteenth century, is packaged so as to allude to the scene from Fellini's film.

Some, however, remain resolutely impervious to the charms of Rome and are pleased – or so they say – to leave the Eternal City:

Road

Ambrose Bierce

All roads, howsoe'er they diverge, lead to Rome,
Whence, thank the good Lord, at least one leads back home.

In his *Devil's Dictionary* (originally published as *The Cynic's Word Book* in 1906), the American writer Bierce (1842–1914) defined a road as 'a strip of land along which one may pass from where it is too tiresome to be to where it is futile to go' and quoted the lines above, attributing them to one 'Borey the Bald'! Bierce never visited Rome – but his jaundiced view may perhaps be excused by the fact that his father was christened Marcus Aurelius Bierce and his uncle Lucus Verus Bierce!

INDEX OF POEM TITLES

Adonais, *from* 94
Aeneid, The, *from* 25
Amours de Voyage, *from* 20
Appian Way, The 59
Arch of Titus, The 58
Art of Love, The, *from* 29
At Dell'Omo 122
At Rome, 22
At the Pyramid of Cestius 96
Bishop Orders His Tomb at St Praxed's Church, The 78
Caffè Greco 120
Carmina, *from* 33, 34
Childe Harold's Pilgrimage, *from* 69, 91
Church of San Clemente, Rome 76
Crossing the Tiber Island 125
Ecce Homo 124
Elegies, The, *from* (Ovid) 31
Elegies, The, *from* (Propertius) 32
Epigrams, The, *from* 35, 36, 37, 38
Facing the Baths of Caracalla 53
Fold 135
Funeral of Pope Leo XII, The 112
Gramsci's Ashes, *from* 116
Grave of Keats, The 97
Hymn to St Teresa, An, *from* 87
I Will Pass through Piazza di Spagna 119
In Bar Rossi, Via Vicenza 122
In the Gesù 83
In the Protestant Cemetery, Rome 99

Ingenuity of Man, The 113

Italy, *from* 17

Keats-Shelley House: Rome 1909, The 102

Manfred, *from* 71

Meo Patacca, *from* 107

November 59

O Rome 115

Odes, The, *from* 28

On Caesar's Amphitheatre 63

On Leaving for Rome with Thoughts about Goethe 23

On Two Gladiators 65

Palatine, The 60

Paradise Regained, *from* 10

Pillar of Trajan, The 55

Politian, *from* 73

Rhinocerite, The 65

Road 136

Roman Elegies, *from* 15

Rome: in the Café 123

Ruins of Rome, The, *from* (du Bellay) 46

Ruins of Rome, The, *from* (Dyer) 47, 67

S. Cecilia in Trastevere 77

Satires, The, *from* (Juvenal) 40, 127

Satires, The, *from* (Horace) 27

Tears of the Excavator, The, *from* 117

To Caesar, on a Woman's Fighting with a Lion 64

To Emilia Lovatelli 98

To Giovanni da Pistoia 83

To Rome 45

Walks in Rome, *from* 85

INDEX OF AUTHORS AND TRANSLATORS

Bellay, Joachim du 46

Belli, G. G. 112, 113

Berneri, Giuseppe 107

Bierce, Ambrose 136

Browning, Robert 78

Byron, Lord 69, 71, 91

Calverley, C. S. (*Translator*) 28

Carducci, Giosuè 53

Catullus 33, 34

Clough, Arthur Hugh 20, 22

Clucas, Humphrey (*Translator*) 34

Cole, Barry 122

Crashaw, Richard 87

Davison, Francis (*Translator*) 36

Dryden, John (*Translator*) 25, 40, 127

Dyer, John 47, 67

Elliot, Alistair (*Translator*) 53

Francis, Philip (*Translator*) 27

Gittings, Robert 76

Goethe 15

Green, Peter (*Translator*) 131

Greene, James (*Translator*) 9

Guidiccioni, Giovanni 45

Hardy, Thomas 96

Harington, Sir John (*Translator*) 36

Hass, Robert (*Translator*) 120

Horace 27, 28

Hunt, Leigh (*Translator*) 35

Juvenal 40, 127

Kemble, Fanny 98

Killigrew, Henry (*Translator*) 63, 64, 65

Kinsella, Thomas 115

Kirkup, James 99, 124

Kramer, Lotte 23

Laughlin, James 123

Longfellow, Henry Wadsworth (*Translator*) 45

Longhorne, John (*Translator*) 33

MacAfee, Norman (*Translator*) 117

Mahon, Derek (*Translator*) 116

Mandelshtam, Osip 9

Marlowe, Christopher (*Translator*) 31

Martial 35, 36, 37, 38, 63, 64, 65

Martinengo, Luciano (*Translator*) 117

Michelangelo 83

Milosz, Czeslaw 120

Milton, John 10

Morris, Sharon 135

Ovid 29, 31, 131

Oxley, William (*Translator*) 107

Palazzeschi, Aldo 59, 60

Pasolini, Pier Paolo 116, 117

Pavese, Cesare 119

Pecke, Thomas (*Translator*) 65

Poe, Edgar Allan 73

Porter, Peter 125

Prince, F. T. 85

Propertius 32

Riley, Peter 77

Rodd, James Rennell 102

Rogers, Samuel 17

Sala, George (*Translator*) 36

Shelley, Percy Bysshe 94

Shepherd, W. G. (*Translator*) 32

Sherburne, Sir Edward (*Translator*) 37

Spenser, Edmund (*Translator*) 46

Stevenson, Robert Louis (*Translator*) 38

Stocks, Mike (*Translator*) 112, 113

Symonds, John Addington (*Translator*) 83

Tomlinson, Charles 83

Vere, Aubrey de 58, 59

Virgil 25

Wilde, Oscar 97

Wolferston, Francis (*Translator*) 29

Wordsworth, William 55

ACKNOWLEDGEMENTS

We would like to thank all of the authors for making this collection possible by allowing us to use their material, and gratefully acknowledge permission to reprint copyright material as follows:

Angel Books, for the extract by Osip Mandelshtam, translated by James Greene; Rockingham Press for 'On Leaving Rome with Thoughts about Goethe' from *The Phantom Lane* by Lotte Kramer (Rockingham Press, 2000); Alistair Elliot for 'Facing the Baths of Caracalla' by Giosuè Garducci; The Society of Authors as the literary representative of the Estate of Robert Gittings for 'Church of San Clemente, Rome'; Carcanet Press Limited for 'Santa Cecilia in Trastevere' from *Selected Poems* by Peter Riley; Anvil Press Poetry for 'Walks in Rome by F. T. Prince; James Kirkup for his own poems 'In the Protestant Cemetary, Rome' and 'Ecce Homo Pier Paolo Pasolini: Report on an Inquest'; William Oxley for his translation of 'Meo Patacca' by Giuseppe Berneri, made especially for this book; Mike Stocks for his translations of 'The Funeral of Pope Leo XII' and 'The Ingenuity of Man' by G. G. Belli; The Gallery Press and Derek Mahon for the translation of 'Gramsci's Ashes' by Pier Paolo Pasonlini; Barry Cole for his poems 'In Bar Rossi, Via Vicenza' and 'At Dell'Omo'; Peter Porter for his poem 'Crossing the Tiber Island'; David Higham Associates for Peter Green's translation from *Ovid – The Poems of Exile*; Enitharmon Press for 'Fold' by Sharon Morris, from her collection *False Spring* (Enitharmon Press 2007).

Every effort has been made to trace or contact copyright holders. The publishers would be pleased to rectify any omissions brought to their notice at the earliest opportunity.

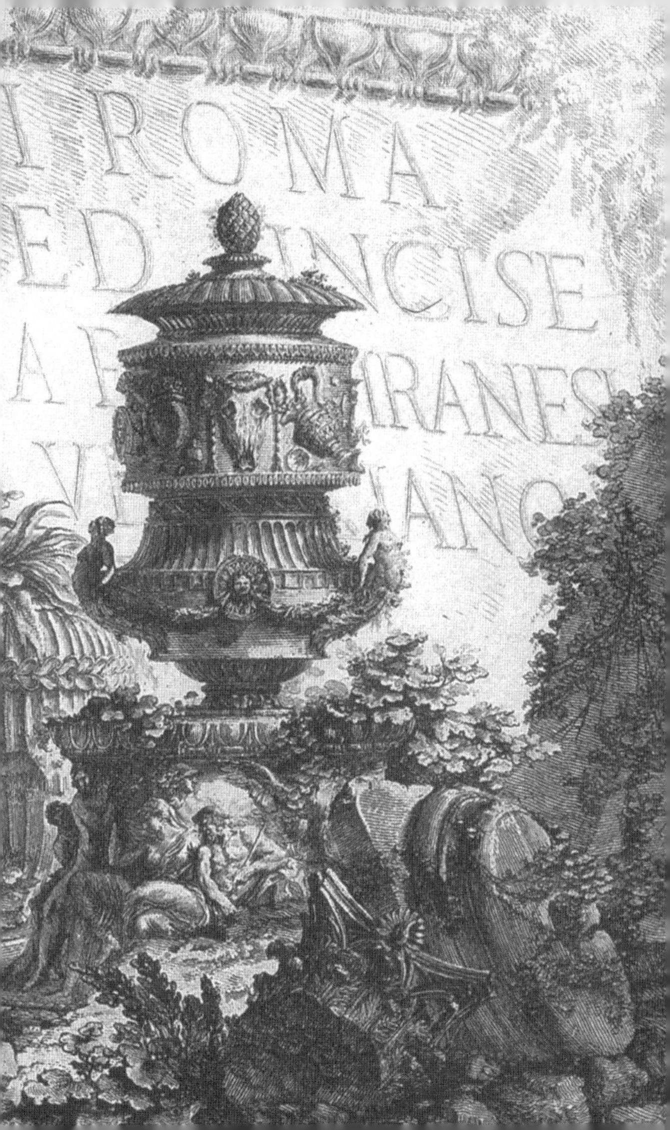
ROMA
ED
NCISE
IRANES
ANO